Why Good Coaches Quit

Why Good Coaches Quit

AND HOW YOU CAN STAY IN THE GAME

John R. Anderson

and

Rick A. Aberman, Ph.D.

Fairview Press
Minneapolis

Published by Fairview Press, 2450 Riverside Avenue South, Minneapolis, MN 55454.

Library of Congress Cataloging-in-Publication Data
Anderson, John, 1955 May 16–
      Why good coaches quit—and how you can stay in the game /
      by John Anderson and Rick Aberman
          p.   cm
      ISBN 1-57749-067-3 (pbk. : alk. paper)
      1. Coaching (Athletics)—United States—Psychological aspects.
  2. Coaches (Athletics)—United States—Family relationships.
  3. Coach-athlete relationships—United States. 4. University of Minnesota—
Baseball.   I. Aberman, Rick Alan. II. Title.
  GV711.A63   1999
  796'.07'7—DC21   98-50806
                                                  CIP

First Printing: September 1999

Printed in the United States of America
02 01 00 99   7 6 5 4 3 2 1

Cover: *Cover Design by Laurie Ingram Duren™*
Text design: Dorie McClelland, Spring Type & Design

For a free current catalog of Fairview Press titles, call toll-free 1-800-544-8207.

Acknowledgments

This book was written for all those who have taken the risk of following their passions, particularly their passion for coaching. There's a kind of craziness involved in pursuing a passion for coaching, but we think that can be healthy. Ideally, our interactions with athletes and our involvement in the business of sports help us understand ourselves better and contribute positively to our personal growth. Our goal in writing this book is to help you see that you are more than you think you are. If we can do that, then we know you that you will try harder. For us this is what leadership and coaching is all about.

We both have an extensive network of people who have touched our lives, and we have depended on many of these people to help us bring our ideas to print.

Bob Livingston, with his uncanny ability to take what we said and have it make sense, was the glue that held the project together. His dedication, hard work, and many talents are testament to the fine person he is. We are truly grateful for his commitment.

Johnny Thompson has been a friend and enthusiastic promoter from the very beginning. Rick Telander is a good friend, columnist, and noted author. We appreciate his helping us see the obvious. We are grateful for the contributions of Jim Frey, Dean of the College of Liberal Arts at the University of Nevada-Las Vegas. His work on positive deviance has given us a language to help us make sense of an important component in competitive sports.

Networks are critical to any successful undertaking. Gratitude goes to Sid Hartman for giving us access to his. Special thanks to Ron Simon, attorney and advisor in Minneapolis, and to Ron Shapiro, attorney and advisor in Baltimore. We also want to thank Malcom Reid and especially Mike Flom, a friend and true professional. We have relied on them for their honesty, integrity, and expertise.

John: The people I work with day-to-day deserve special mention. Among these people, of course, are the athletes. It's difficult to be an effective teacher without good students. In addition, three people have stood out in making this project a success: Diane Ficenko, my secretary, and two valued assistant coaches, Rob Fournasier and Mike Dee, who is now the Head Baseball Coach at the University of Illinois-Chicago. I am also grateful to my former college coaches, Dick Siebert and George Thomas, who faithfully demonstrated their belief in me. To Jan and Erin Anderson, who encouraged and supported me in this project. And to my parents, LeRoy and Mary Ann, who were my first and best coaches. They trusted me to find the right answers to life's challenges in my own way. They were always available when I needed some fresh perspective to help me grow. Regretfully, my father passed away before the book was published. I will miss his valued feedback.

Rick: Many of the stories included in this book were made possible by the numerous athletes and coaches who have allowed me to become part of their lives. One coach in particular deserves special thanks. Karen Parker has contributed to this project in more ways than she will ever realize. You know how important it is for me to feel your presence. The ideas of my former teacher and mentor Carl Whitaker, M.D., have shaped my professional world and are reflected here. He helped me see the importance of being connected to my self. I have also been fortunate to have an informal "cuddle group" consisting of my dad, Bill Aberman, and my brother, David. The daily lunches we have shared have helped keep me grounded in reality. My mother, Bailee Aberman, passed away suddenly during the project. Her belief in me was just about the best thing a parent could ever provide.

John Anderson
Rick Aberman

Contents

"WE CAN'T SOLVE PROBLEMS
BY USING THE SAME KIND OF THINKING
AS WE USED WHEN WE CREATED THEM."

–ALBERT EINSTEIN

Introduction

THE OTHER STUFF

Duke basketball coach Mike Krzyzewski spoke for many coaches, amateur and professional, when he said, "The coaching, I love. The kids, I love. It's the other stuff you have to watch out for." Watching out for The Other Stuff is what this book is all about.

Men and women who go into coaching are generally prepared to handle game strategies and fundamentals—the "Xs and Os" of the sport. At least, they know what's expected of them in this regard. What coaches don't expect is The Other Stuff. Few coaches, for example, are prepared to have a player walk up to them and say, "Coach, I'm pregnant. Should I get an abortion?" No amount of knowledge about athletic technique can address the medical, legal, and ethical responsibilities such a question raises. Likewise, nothing in most coaches' training prepares them for the arrest of their star player after he has assaulted his girlfriend—again. What do you do if you learn about the assault, not from the player himself, but from a reporter? What are your responsibilities to the player? the team? the victim? the community?

How do you motivate players who are more concerned about sports bags, travel opportunities, and other special perks than improving the quality of their game? How do you cope with parents who accuse you of being a lousy coach and ruining their child's chances for a scholarship or a pro contract? How do you balance the demands of coaching with the responsibilities you have to your spouse and your own kids?

Welcome to The Other Stuff and the new realities of coaching. They're driving experienced coaches nuts and causing almost every coach to wonder whether coaching is worth it or not.

We're All in the Business

Whether you coach a town hockey team, a workplace softball team, a high school football squad, or a major university basketball program, you face many of the same problems. In these days of traveling "B" teams for eight-year-olds, even volunteer coaches of "non-revenue" sports must deal to some degree with the business of sports. As soon as you hold tryouts, as soon as you start raising money, as soon as the local paper writes about your team, you are into The Other Stuff. You, the coach, are under pressures not directly connected with teaching kids how to play the game.

The hard truth is that coaches who ignore The Other Stuff often end up out of the game. Either they are fired because they fail to accomplish some major objective of their program, or they quit because they are overwhelmed by off-the-field pressures.

While we can't provide you with easy answers to the complex issues facing coaches today—no "how-to" or "ten easy steps" panaceas—we can offer the insights of people who have been around the business a long time and still find joy in coaching. Successful coaches are those who have learned how to strike a balance between field operations and The Other Stuff. We wrote this book to help you learn how to strike your own balance as a coach. In this book we will identify some of the potential pitfalls of modern coaching. We'll give you insights into effective management techniques that you can use in any sport, at any level. And we'll share with you some examples of how other coaches have successfully handled The Other Stuff.

The book is divided into five main sections. The first focuses on the coach as an individual. The second treats the coach's relationship with his or her family. The third section looks at the larger world of coaching and the issues coaches commonly face. The fourth section illustrates these issues with real-life examples. The final chapter returns the focus to the individual and pulls together the main themes of the book.

With some obvious exceptions, the examples used in this book represent composites of several people rather than actual case histories. The exceptions include a series of examples offered by John Anderson, based on his personal experiences as Head Baseball Coach at the University of Minnesota. Throughout the book, John comments from this "head coach" perspective. Rick Aberman, in turn, offers his unique perspective as a psychologist—a "head head coach."

The good news is that you are not alone. There are thousands of men and women out there who are facing the same problems, the same dilemmas, and the same pressures you are. However daunting these problems, dilemmas, and pressures may seem, we believe that coaching is still one of the most important things a person can do, whether as an amateur or a professional. We hope you agree. Our kids and our sports need good coaches like you.

Section One

Coaching and You

Career-killing Conflicts

Most of us get into coaching because we have a passion for our sport and a desire to pass our knowledge on to others. For some of us, coaching may be the only way to continue to participate in a sport after injury or age has brought our playing days to an end. For others of us, coaching may offer an opportunity, often as a volunteer, to become more involved with our children. And for a growing number of men and women studying coaching in formal college and university programs, coaching is a primary career goal.

Whatever the reason for getting into coaching, few if any neophyte coaches are adequately prepared to deal with the off-the-field pressures of organized sports—what we are calling The Other Stuff. Take ex-athletes, for example. While it's not uncommon for former players to have observed the game preparation strategies of their mentors and the tactics used to win on the field, athletes are rarely privy to the strategies and tactics of winning the equally important game that's played off the field.

The same goes for those parents who volunteer to coach their child's team. Most are unprepared to handle the off-the-field problems that can come with coaching youth sports: highly competitive community athletic associations, intractable governing boards, meddlesome parents, and misbehaving kids. The shock of having to deal with such problems causes over half of new volunteer coaches to either quit in the middle of a season or refuse to return for a second season.

Even college-trained coaches receive little preparation for handling The Other Stuff. While some institutions are beginning to teach the psychological aspects of performance enhancement, or are requiring finance and negotiating courses as part of their curriculum, few if any are training coaches how to recognize and deal with the everyday problems of coaching today's athletes in today's world.

Because of this lack of preparation, many coaches, professional as well as amateur, are quickly overwhelmed by the non-sports-related demands made on them by athletes, parents, administrators, and others. To stay in the game, a coach must learn to deal effectively with The Other Stuff.

JOHN ANDERSON

"I started coaching at age twenty-five—not much older than my players—with no head coaching experience, and all of a sudden I was running a major university baseball program. I was thrown in the fire and had to try to define who I was and what my philosophy was as I went along. I think I did pretty well with the field operations part of the job: teaching proper technique and managing the games. But I had no clue how to handle the financial, public relations, and personal issues. I had never been through a budgeting cycle; the media constantly hammered me, saying I was a lousy coach; parents called me an idiot for not playing their kids more; and I didn't know what to do for kids whose problems off the field affected their performance. I began to believe that maybe I wasn't cut out for coaching.

"Over time I've learned to be more comfortable dealing with the press and with the financial part of my job because it was in my best interest to do so, especially if I had any hopes of staying in coaching at this level. I had to learn or leave. I'm still trying to learn about The Other Stuff, but every year there seem to be new hurdles. I think I'm doing okay, but I'm never sure."

RICK ABERMAN

"Coaches often come to me in frustration. They say, 'Doc, am I crazy, or is it the system? I'm starting to feel like maybe it's me.' I tell them, no, it's not you. What you're feeling is normal. It's really the system that's screwed up. You see, when you try to operate rationally in an irrational system, you feel crazy, trapped. You don't know what to do, so you internalize the conflict and blame it on yourself. I try to help coaches see that what they're feeling is normal. It's okay."

Striking a Balance Between Coaching and the Rest of Your Life

PASSION AND BUSINESS

You have a passion for the game or you wouldn't be coaching. You got into coaching because that's what you wanted to do. You're a winner. You're prepared. You like kids. You like to teach. You want to make a difference in kids' lives.

Many coaches say, "For me, 2:30 p.m. is the best time of the day, because that's when I go to practice. Then I can coach, I can teach. And, at least for a little while, I don't have to put up with The Other Stuff."

You may be comfortable with field operations, but you also have to understand The Other Stuff. It's part of your job, and if you don't understand it, it's going to blindside you. Coaching on the field is just one part of your job. You've got to recruit, address the problems that kids bring with them from home, and interact with the hierarchy of power in your athletic organization. You also have to reconcile your responsibilities as a coach with your responsibilities outside the game.

Relationships and Coaching

There is an aphorism about coaching: "There's no clock, no calendar, and no vacation in this business."

John:
"One Christmas vacation, my family and I were visiting my in-laws, and I had to leave a couple of days early to come back to campus to meet with a player and his family. The parents had demanded the meeting at this time, and there were issues we needed to address. My family had a real hard time understanding why I had to cut my vacation short. I had an equally hard time explaining why it was a necessary part of my job. No one talks about how to prepare for this stuff. If you're not very careful about managing the whole of your life, it's easy to get trapped into a situation where the job becomes all-consuming."

Imagine that you have volunteered to coach your eight-year-old's team. You spend a lot of time figuring out how you will organize practice, what skills you will teach the kids, and what game strategies you want to use. You think you have everything under control, when, all of a sudden, on the first day of practice, a parent confronts you and says, "My kid better play just as much as the other kids, or you'll hear from me!"

Now practice is over, and all of the kids have been picked up except one. You can't leave, but your family and dinner are waiting for you. You know you're going to hear, "Why is it your job to baby-sit that kid? Practice is over at 5:00. You're not the kid's parent."

Many times, even the people most important to us don't understand that there is more to being a coach than practices and games. And yet when your family asks, "What do you care more about—coaching or us," you share their frustration. When you signed up to coach, you didn't know you were going to have to deal with all this Other Stuff. You just want to go home on time and enjoy your life off the field like everyone else.

To stay in the game, coaches have to learn to balance their coaching life and their family life. The balance point isn't the same for everyone. Some coaches may even feel forced to choose between coaching and having a relationship. This is especially the case for professionals, who, in the first few years on the job, spend much of their time traveling with the team or working at the office. Some younger coaches decide to sacrifice everything for their career. Then they reach their mid-thirties and realize that they've never had a serious relationship and the clock is ticking down for starting a family. Many female coaches leave the profession mid-career for just this reason.

YOU AND COACHING

Coaching can be seductive. One successful season, and suddenly everyone is identifying the coach with the championship team. But what happens if the next season the team doesn't win the championship? Those who once glorified the coach as a genius can just as quickly vilify him or her as a failure. If the coach has come to view him or herself through the lens of public approval, the turnabout can be devastating.

To stay in the game, coaches need to define themselves as people first, coaches second. What really matters is not some title or label you've taken on, but who you are as a person. Unfortunately, it's a lot easier to say this than it is to put it into practice. There are not many places coaches can go to get help and advice. Other, more experienced, coaches can be excellent resources, but many coaches are reluctant to admit to their peers that they have problems or weaknesses. This may be especially true for female or minority coaches, who may already feel that they're being judged more harshly than their majority counterparts.

The irony is that even as coaching challenges your sense of self-identity, it threatens to rob you of the time you may need to resolve personal issues. On-field operations take up only a fraction of your total time spent coaching. The Other Stuff takes up the rest. And, of course, the time spent dealing with The Other Stuff comes right out of the rest of your life.

Isn't it Really About the Kids?

NEED VS. WANT—WHY DO KIDS PLAY?

Coaches today often complain about kids no longer having a passion for the game. But it's hard to be passionate when you feel you have to do something, that you don't have any choice about whether you do it or not. Some kids feel they have to play sports because, if they quit, their parents would think that they didn't love them or appreciate the sacrifices that had been made for them. Some families seem to be close only because of their children's participation in sports. Without the practices, the games, the trips, the whole culture of sports, the family wouldn't have much in common to talk about or look forward to.

No athlete can play up to his or her full potential without the freedom to choose not to play at all. If you feel that you can quit, then you are making a choice: you're playing because you want to play. If you are just trying to live up to someone else's expectations, you're playing because you need to play.

Ask almost any youngster why he or she plays a particular sport, and you will hear, "Because it's fun." Ask many parents why their kids are involved in sports, and you will get more complex answers about learning experiences, character building, and opportunities for self-betterment.

What happens when playing a sport isn't fun for a young athlete? The following is, in many ways, a representative example: A kid works hard through high school to win a full athletic scholarship to a Division I university. Not only does he win a scholarship, but, as a freshman, he plays in a national championship game. But to this kid, the big game is no big deal at all—all he wants is to have a life: to go out to dinner with his friends, to see his girlfriend more often, to go to a movie or a play once in a while. Nineteen years old, and he's already burned out on his sport. More than anything else, he wants to quit the team and escape the pressures of big college athletics, but he feels trapped by the investments that other people have made in him—the time and money his parents have spent on him, the scholarship the university gave him, the training his coaches have given him.

As a coach, it's easy to get caught in the middle of a situation like this. You've worked hard to get to a championship, and suddenly, inexplicably, your star player doesn't seem to care anymore. What can you do to avoid this sort of frustration?

RICK:

"When I really want to figure out what's going on with an athlete, I ask, 'Do you feel that, if you really wanted to, you could quit playing right now and just walk away from the game?' Sometimes, then, the real issues come out and the kid says, 'No, I couldn't quit. You're right, I'm not having fun, I'm not enjoying this. But my parents and coaches would be crushed if I quit after all the money and time they've spent on me, and my friends wouldn't talk to me.' Meanwhile the kid is burned out because he's playing for all the wrong reasons. As a coach you have to keep your eyes open for who is having fun and who is not. Sometimes, with a good player, you may be tempted to look the other way because you want the kid on your team even if he or she is not having a good time.

"Coaches tend to assume that kids play because they want to, and that can be a mistake. To be successful over the long term, coaches need to develop the skills to probe their players' motives and prepare accordingly."

Many of the problems kids face as they advance competitively in their sport involve trying to live up to the expectations other people have for them—their parents, their coaches, their community. In the beginning, the kids play because it's fun. But then other agendas intervene. Some parents tie their social life, even their self-esteem, to their child's sports career. They may rationalize that what they're doing is for the child's sake, that they're just encouraging or helping the child do what he or she really wants to do. But, too often, what the parents are doing is for their own sake. They've stopped communicating with their kids when they should be probing, listening, and helping them formulate healthy reasons for playing.

JOHN:
"I remember a fourteen-year-old boy who attended one of my summer camps. His main reason for playing baseball was to get a major college scholarship. Why? Because his dad had told him he had to. That may be a kind of motivation, but it's not a very healthy one.

"Too many parents push their child to play sports for their reasons rather than the child's reasons. They never really ask the child what he or she wants; they just keep pushing the child along assuming that's what he or she wants. Then the child feels an obligation to the parents to continue.

"Coaches become involved in the parent-child relationship whether or not they want to. We need to determine a kid's motivation early in our relationship. It's as much for our sanity as for theirs."

ENTITLEMENT VS. ACCOUNTABILITY AND RESPONSIBILITY

More than a few coaches have lamented that they are fed up with the attitudes of some of their athletes—kids who seem to feel that they're entitled to their position on the team, their scholarship, their lifestyle, just because they have been told since early childhood that they are special.

Here's the sort of thing that these coaches are seeing: A high school football player is passed along academically because he is needed on the field. When he gets to college, he still expects to be allowed to perform on the field regardless of how he performs in the classroom. The athlete may be eighteen, nineteen, twenty years old, and yet no one has ever challenged his sense of entitlement or demanded some personal responsibility.

Coaches generally see it as their duty to try to instill responsible habits in their players. Be at a certain place at a certain time. Take care of your equipment. Help set up before practice. Pick up the team equipment after practice. From the youth leagues to the pros, however, today's players are typically perceived to be less accountable and responsible than those of previous generations. It used to be taken for granted that teaching kids responsibility was a parent's job. Now, it's not uncommon for a parent to tell a coach, "It's your job to teach my kid responsibility. That's what this sports thing is all about, isn't it?"

Is it surprising, then, that more and more coaches, especially volunteer coaches, are saying, "The hell with it, I didn't sign up to be a baby sitter. I don't need this Stuff," and are leaving the game?

DEPENDENCE VS. INDEPENDENCE

There is another aspect to the notion of accountability that can also create frustration for coaches. In most books and courses on coaching, building strong and independent young people is high on the list of goals. When the coach goes out into the real world, however, the pressure to succeed, to win at all costs, sometimes pushes the coach in exactly the opposite direction. "Do as you're told," the coach barks at the team. "I'll decide what's best for you."

Certainly, in team sports a player needs to put team ahead of self, but no player should be forced into a state of dependence. Unfortunately, that's what is happening to many players, sometimes from an early age. In some of the larger youth sport organizations, the kid's time is structured down to the minute, and the kid becomes totally dependent on the coach, the chaperone, or the community official. No one seems to consider how such absolute control might inhibit the growth of the child's ability to think and act independently and responsibly. We need scrutinize ourselves and our programs and ask: "Are we doing what we're doing for the good of the player or the good of the business? For the needs of the child or the needs of the coach?" Kids won't have all the answers, but they deserve to be given the chance to have some input in how decisions affecting them are made.

We need to pay attention to what we are teaching both on the field and off. Out of our desire to succeed, we inadvertently teach dependency by over-coaching. And yet, our role, by definition, is to help and teach young people–to coach them—not do it for them. We can open a door, but the kids have to walk through it on their own. In this way, we act as facilitators to learning, as consultants. Teaching dependency is one of the worst things we can do as a coach.

In the short run, teaching our players to think and do for themselves may not help win more games. But in the long run, the key to sustained optimal performance is to get athletes to think independently and make good decisions. Having players take ownership of their situation ultimately means less work and less stress for you, the coach, and better performance from the players. You'll find that your time-spent to benefits-received ratio will improve significantly.

Whose Interests Are Being Served?

THE BUSINESS OF SPORTS

Sports is big business. At every level of competition—from amateur to professional, youth leagues to adult leagues—sports is a financial enterprise in which business values often come into direct confrontation with other values. And the coach is the person most often caught in the middle between these conflicting values. How, for example, does a coach balance the need to educate student-athletes against the demands of alumni who value only winning? Or the need to protect the health and safety of children against a sports association's limited budget for equipment and maintenance?

What's good for the player often has little to do with what's good for the business of sports. What's good for the player is what helps him or her grow as a person as well as an athlete. Independence, responsibility, fairness, team play, and good sportsmanship are the values that coaches have traditionally tried to instill in their players. Business, on the other hand, sometimes promotes values of a very different sort: dependence on authority rather than independence and responsibility, expedience rather than fairness and good sportsmanship, self-interest rather than team play.

INJURIES VS. WINNING

For years the unwritten rule for coaches at every level of sports was, "Put the health of the player first. Don't risk further injury by allowing someone to play hurt." Today we see the pressures of winning pushing coaches to make decisions that have nothing to do with the welfare of the player and everything to do with the bottom line. Too often, coaches are exploiting the competitive drive of their players by exhorting them to "play through the pain."

An injured player, particularly a young child, often does not have the ability to decide if he or she is fit to play. The decision of whether or not a player should return to competition from an injury must be made by a competent independent source: a physician or trainer. The coach who ignores a physician's or trainer's recommendation and tells a kid to "just run it off" is risking not only further injury to the player, but a lawsuit that could ruin the coach's reputation and career.

THE RECRUITING GAME

Let's be blunt. The high school player who gets a university athletic scholarship is getting paid to play, though most coaches would avoid saying so directly. When coaches recruit a prospect for their team, they entice the player, and the player's parents, to sign a letter of intent by emphasizing the opportunities the player will have to grow as a person. They tell the parents, "We are here for your child. We'll take care of him." Or, "Of course your daughter will have a well-rounded university experience. We'll see to that." Then the kid gets to campus and very quickly begins to think: "Hey, these people don't really care about me, they just want to win."

It would be in the player's best interest, and ultimately our own, if we could be more honest in this process. We should tell the player and the player's parents up front that the scholarship is basically a business arrangement, a contract. The player is receiving a consideration—a college scholarship—and with that consideration comes responsibility and sacrifice. Yes, there will be many enriching educational opportunities for the student-athlete on campus. But in return for these opportunities, the student-athlete will be required to attend regular classes, as well as special study and tutoring programs in the athletic department, because academic eligibility must be maintained. The student-athlete may participate in extra-curricular campus activities as time permits, but sports is a year-round activity and comes first. The athletic department can provide payment in the form of a scholarship, but it can't take care of the student-athlete's every want and need. Although the business relationship isn't as obvious in college as it is in professional sports, it's still a business relationship, and the student-athlete is part of the business enterprise.

The Inescapable Conclusion

It's obvious that there are many forces out there threatening your ability to accomplish your goals as a coach. No wonder so many good coaches are quitting every day.

What can you do to keep your perspective while dealing with these issues and conflicts? How can you help instill values in your players while meeting the demands of the business-side of your sport? How can you survive and thrive as a coach in the real world of modern sports?

One of the most important things you can do is to try to develop a better understanding of yourself: your values, your tendencies, your methods of operation as a coach. Self-knowledge is the foundation on which successful coaches build their careers. Without a strong sense of who you are, both as a person and a coach, your chances of staying in the game are slim at best.

But Who Would I Be if I Wasn't a Coach?

Often, the job we're doing defines us before we can define the job. This is certainly true in the field of coaching, where The Other Stuff sometimes not only defines the job but redefines it when we least expect it.

In a story published in the Providence Journal-Bulletin, 1998 Olympic gold medal-winning goalie Sarah Tueting described how her interest in hockey diminished during her sophomore year in college. She was afraid to quit playing, though, because, as she put it, "Hockey had become such a big part of my identity." Though Tueting was speaking as a player, her situation applies to many coaches. If you have ever thought, "I can't handle this Stuff—but who would I be if I quit coaching?" you have let the job define you. You're not alone. If you are totally consumed with coaching (and the good ones usually are), it's possible to lose perspective on other aspects of your life and, ultimately, on coaching itself.

As we noted earlier, in a world as obsessed with sports as ours, it's easy to be seduced by the attention and approval that success in sports so readily attracts. A coach is likely to see other facets of his or her life overlooked or minimized as he or she becomes more successful. The tendency, then, is believe your own press clippings and to base your self-identity on your successes—and failures—as a coach. When this happens, you're letting the job define you. And should The Other Stuff intervene, as it so often does, to redefine your job, you may be faced with an identity crisis, no matter how successful you have been in the past.

Make It Your Own

Allowing the job to define you is one way to invite a crisis into your coaching career. Another way, especially for less experienced coaches, is to pattern your program after someone else's coaching style and philosophy, and not your own. Coaching by imitation is an easy way to get started, and we can all learn from the successful coaches who've gone before us; but blindly applying a system and set of standards that worked well in one situation to a new and completely different set of circumstances is a prescription for disaster. As difficult as it may be, good coaches must design systems that fit their personality and style of teaching. And to stay in the game, coaches must be willing to modify or replace a system, even their own.

People get thrust into this business at all levels without much experience. If you start out using familiar tools, that's fine. But it's important to stop once in a while and ask, "Does this system fit who I am, my goals, my values, and my sense of the kind of coach I want to be? What kind of program fits my personality and skills and the personality and skills of the team I'm coaching? Is that the kind of program I'm running?"

RICK:

"When I work with coaches, I tell them about their mental map. Everything you do is informed by the sum total of your personal experiences: your mental map. Your mental map guides your thinking in many ways, not just in the way you coach. Your most destructive prejudices and your most honorable ideals are both parts of the geography of your mental map.

"When you first start out in coaching, your mental map, at least as it relates to coaching, is relatively constricted, and it is natural for you to stay within safe and familiar boundaries. As you gain experience, however, your mental map should begin to broaden and change. You are taking a system that you inherited and making it our own. If your mental map remains static, it means that you are not learning from your successes and failures. You are not making that familiar old system your own.

"You need to take ownership of a philosophy, system, or style and remake it based on your own background, experiences, and talents. If your coaching style doesn't reflect who you are, it's shallow and insincere, and kids will quickly read you as a phony."

JOHN:

"You can make an analogy with the way kids emulate famous athletes. The kids think, 'Gee, Frank Thomas wears Reebok, and he's my hero, so I have to have them, too.' Or, 'Kobe Bryant wears Adidas, and I want to be like him.' But there are a lot of good shoes out there, and some will be better fits than others, regardless of who endorses them. As a coach, you need to study all your options, then choose what's best for your situation. That doesn't mean you can't borrow from a coach you admire. It's adopting an entire program, without any modifications or customizing, that can cause problems for a coach.

"You have to ask, 'Does this work for me? Do I have the resources, equipment, and athletes to implement this type of program? Forget the other guy—what's my situation?'"

It's easy for any coach, not just the neophyte, to become caught up in a vicious cycle. You copy one coach's successful program. It doesn't work for you, so you copy someone else. When that doesn't work, you copy someone else. Or, the system you are now using isn't working as well as it once did, so you import an entirely different system from a more successful program. And when that system doesn't meet your expectations, you're out looking for yet another system to import. You need to break the cycle and look inside instead of outside.

Coaches sometimes forget that athletes are an integral part of any coaching system. If you copy a program whose success depends on the speed of its athletes and your team is built for power, that program probably isn't going to work for your team no matter how successful it's been elsewhere. Do you even have access to the type of athlete that makes the other program work?

Beginning coaches usually have little coaching experience and little time to prepare, so it's no wonder that they often fall back on a system they learned during their playing days. Starting from a familiar mental map isn't a problem; staying frozen in a mental map is. To stay in the game, you have to be prepared to adapt and change from the very first minute of the very first practice.

I Don't Need to Put Up with This Stuff

The easy thing to do when confronted with The Other Stuff is to quit. Good coaches quit every day.

For almost every coach, there comes a time when The Other Stuff seems overwhelming. During such a crisis, a coach can either crash and burn, or recover and go on to a fulfilling career.

We are going to look now at three examples of coaches facing such crises: a former star athlete just starting out in coaching, an experienced coach taking over a new program, and the near-legendary coach of a major university program facing new challenges. At the end of each example, we will give you our thoughts about the stresses that can create such a crisis and some possible strategies to resolve it. There are no "right" answers, no simple panaceas. As you read each example, try to place yourself in the coach's situation as much as possible. What would you do? How would you handle the situation? How can you incorporate what these coaches have learned into your mental map?

Joan: Imitate Until They Drop

Joan Lacey is in her third year as a soccer coach. Only twenty-six years old, she entered the coaching ranks directly after finishing her university playing career. Her first two years were spent as head coach of a large suburban high school where she was hired to turn girls soccer from an intramural sport into a varsity program. This season, she is an assistant coach at a small college in another area.

Joan played high school soccer at the time when opportunities for girls to play at a competitive, varsity level were exploding. She learned her basic skills from her father, who had been an All-American at a major soccer power in the Midwest. The game came easily to Joan; she was strong, intelligent, and quick. She started for her high school as a ninth-grader and was an All-State center forward by the time she was a junior.

Thirty-eight colleges and universities recruited Joan. She accepted a full scholarship at a university that had one of the best soccer programs in the country. The coach was a major builder of the sport for women, and Joan felt honored to play for him. She repeated her high school success in college and equaled her father's achievement by being named an All-American in her senior year. Soccer was Joan's joy and reason for being.

The end of her playing days came as a shock to Joan Lacey. Her team lost to a lightly regarded opponent in the first round of playoffs. Immediately, her playing career was finished. She never even considered playing club soccer after starring at such a high level. The national team had already been chosen, and there was no pro game for women. The day after her final game, Joan wandered out of habit to the soccer field at the regular practice time. It was empty.

As the initial shock wore off, Joan began to think for the first time about coaching. She approached her college coach about a graduate assistant position, but none was open. It was at this time that the athletic director of a prestigious private high school in an affluent suburb close by called her.

"Ms. Lacey, I was at the game and was stunned when the team lost. I've been a big fan of yours since you were a freshman, and I'm sorry your playing days were cut short. But perhaps we have a situation that can help you stay in the game and help us get a varsity-level girls soccer program off the ground. Are you interested?"

After Joan had asked many questions, she was curious enough to arrange a formal visit to the school. During her interview, Joan was impressed with both the quality of the athletic facilities and the size of the budget she would control. She knew she couldn't make ends meet on her salary from this job alone, but the athletic director had already taken care of that. A prominent alumnus owned a small chain of high-end sporting goods stores, and Joan would be most welcome to work in one of the stores on a part-time basis during the season and full-time when her coaching schedule permitted. Between the two jobs, Joan felt she could pay her bills.

Joan made it very clear to the athletic director that she had no coaching experience and was a bit apprehensive about taking on head coaching responsibilities and building a program from scratch. The athletic director reassured her by saying, "I know the program you just played for. Your university coach is world famous and you were a talented player. You can lean on all that while you build this program." Joan accepted the offer and moved to her new community immediately. The athletic director arranged a press conference to introduce Joan as "a great player, an All-American player. She has played for the best of programs and under the best of coaches and systems. Now she will lead our girls' soccer program to greatness as its first head coach."

Lacey spent the month before fall practice intensely reviewing everything she had learned in her college career. She talked to her former coach, and he sent her a copy of his workout schedule and playbook. Joan was thrilled and gratified by his support. Her university team was known for its conditioning, speed, passing skills and an aggressive defense that relied on precise execution. Joan decided if her former coach's system had been a good enough methodology for the university team, it was good enough for her.

At her first practice, thirty-eight kids turned out, twenty of them with club level experience at the school and two transfers with previous varsity experience, including a goalkeeper. Joan started the session just the way she had been taught—with stretching exercises followed by wind sprints. The obviously poor physical conditioning of many of the players disturbed her, but she vowed to make sure that would not a problem by the time the season started.

Next came the passing drills. They were a shambles. Many of the girls had no idea how to pass the ball to a stationary player, let alone lead a moving one. Joan spent most of her time on the field running from one group to another, demonstrating her passing skills and hoping to teach by example. But passing a ball herself and teaching the mechanics of passing to someone else, as it turned out, were two very different things. At the end of that first practice, the girls were confused, bedraggled, and depressed. "Well," Joan thought, "we need to keep to the plan and things will work out."

By the end of the three-week practice period, over half the girls had quit or were hurt. Nothing serious, but a lot of strains and pulls. Joan still had enough players to field a team, but the group were slow and underskilled in passing and playmaking. Joan made some modifications and simplifications to her college playbook but, for the most part, kept her former coach's system intact.

That first season was the worst experience of Joan's athletic life. The team didn't win a single game and managed only two ties, both against a school also in its premier year of competition. The athletic director told her not to worry; it was, after all, the first year of the program. During the winter, Joan attended a coaching clinic run by her former coach. She learned a number of new strategies and techniques, but, of course, they were still based on her old coach's system. Also during the off-season, Joan got herself into as good shape as possible so she could demonstrate her techniques to the team, not just tell them. The summer conditioning program she had given the returning players and her more hands-on approach surely would turn things around.

The second year was a dismal repeat of the first. Joan's program emphasizing speed and footwork broke down when forced on players who were relatively slow. The defense got a bit stronger, but the end result was only one win and three ties. This time, the athletic director was not nearly as kind or encouraging. He suggested that Joan had better turn things around the next season or they would have to consider a coaching change.

Joan was dejected and confused. How could such a successful system fail so miserably? It had to be her fault; she was not implementing the system properly. She called Sue Evans, the former captain of her university team who was now coaching a small college program. After several long telephone calls, Sue invited Joan to sit in on her practices and games. The college still had a month to go in their season and, with a little luck, the Division III playoffs.

The differences between Joan's program and Sue's startled Joan. She recognized a few of the basics from her university system, but Sue had scrapped much of it, then simplified what was left and adapted that to a group of women who were not scholarship athletes with great natural skills and experience. And she was winning—18-3-3 record, with a real shot at the conference championship. After observing Sue and her program, Joan concluded that she couldn't keep coaching the way she had been, but the problem was that she didn't know any other way to coach. Sue suggested that, if she could afford it, Joan could join her as an assistant coach. The pay was poor, but the town and campus were beautiful, and Joan would have a chance to develop as a coach without the pressures and unrealistic expectations of her current position. Joan accepted. The athletic director at her previous school didn't appear really sorry to see her leave.

In her third year in the profession, Joan finally began to learn to be a coach. Sue's team was very different from the year before, and Sue's coaching technique and program changed with the players. Joan got to be a hands-on teacher for the first time, working specifically with the offensive players. She began to add her own touches to Sue's program, with the head coach's enthusiastic permission. At the end of the season, Joan felt she had made more progress as an assistant that year than in her two previous years as an ill-prepared, "copycat" coach.

JOHN:

"Even though a particular system or coaching philosophy can produce a national champion in one situation, it can produce a disaster in another. Players have different skills, different commitments, and different agendas. You just can't take a program you may have played under and export it without change.

"I know of a situation where a guy who had played under a really tough college basketball coach, one who took physical conditioning and sticking to a rigid schedule to the extreme, was made coach of a junior high team. He spent a considerable amount of time before practice putting together the fifteen things he wanted to accomplish that day. He would never even get to the second thing in practice, though, because the kids would be worn out after performing conditioning drills designed for much older athletes in much better condition. His mental map had not prepared him for the change in age group and skill level.

"You have to go into any coaching situation, whether it is your first year or your thirtieth year, and make the program your own. Take ideas from whomever you want, but work them and tailor them to the realities of the age and ability level of the team you are coaching now. Copying somebody else's system completely and using it in the wrong situation is horrible for the program, the kids, and your career."

RICK:

"For some athletes, getting into coaching is a therapeutic response to the dilemma of 'What do I do now that my playing days are over?' Their identity is all wrapped up in athletic performance. They still feel like a player, but they're no longer on a team, so who are they? Where can they go, and how can they become part of a system again?

"This is an unsettling experience. Like delayed adolescents, they look for something that can prolong their youth. Coaching is often one of those things. You see a lot of young coaches coaching as if they are still players. Internally, that's how they feel. Hopefully, they will come to see coaching as a transition to maturity, not a way to delay it. If you stay in coaching, sooner or later you need to start thinking of yourself not as a player or even a player-coach, but as a coach. Thinking of yourself as a coach is part of the maturation process. So is letting go of the system you played under and developing a system of your own.

"It is really easy to blame the kids when the system isn't working. It's easy to rationalize, 'Hey, the system works at XYZ University. I know the system and I'm applying it exactly the same way they do. It must be the kids not putting out.'

"Remember, you aren't the same coach as the person who put that system together. You have your own strengths and weaknesses. It is impossible for any coach to be exactly like another.

"The system you're emulating may have been devised decades ago. Kids change. What motivated kids even a few years ago may turn them completely off today. Sparky Anderson said once, 'You have to understand the needs of your players. That's got to be your first concern. When I first started, my first concern was me.'

Sparky Anderson had one of the longest and most successful coaching careers in baseball history. If you want to stay in the game, you need to take his words to heart: You have to understand your players before you can make any system work effectively. Learn to listen and to change."

Jacques & the Battle for East High

Jacques Bottiglier is one of those people for whom the cliché "he could skate before he could walk" seemed to have been invented. He grew up in Vermont near the Canadian border. From the age of eight, "Jack Bottle-ear," as he was called, played organized hockey and played it well. Instead of playing high school in the United States, he opted to play in the famed Junior A League of Quebec across the border in Canada.

When he turned eighteen, young Jacques and his parents decided to postpone a professional career, and Jacques accepted a full scholarship from a collegiate hockey power in a northeastern state. During his college career, Bottiglier made all-conference twice as a defenseman and the dean's list several times. He also suffered a series of nagging injuries— not enough to keep him off the ice for long, but enough to make him question the wisdom of a career in pro hockey after graduation.

Instead, Jacques enrolled at another, larger university in New England, where he earned a Master's degree in Education with an emphasis on coaching. He served as an unpaid graduate assistant to Mike Andersen, one of the best college coaches in one of best college programs of the time. Mike became a friend and mentor to Jacques. Jacques later told Mike that he felt the time spent learning from him was the most productive training he could possibly have received.

As he was studying for his graduate degree, Jacques continued to play amateur hockey in a league made up mostly of former college and Junior players, all under age thirty-five. It wasn't the NHL, but for Jacques it was an opportunity to play as well as coach and to stay closely connected to the game he loved.

When Jacques finished his master's, he found his first coaching employment at the high school in his hometown in Vermont—the one he'd chosen not to play for. One of the reasons Jacques had left town was the tawdry arena with its small ice area, bad boards, poor lighting, and non-existent locker rooms. In the decade he'd been away, the community and the school board had passed a bond issue to build a modern ice arena with state-of-the-art facilities. They built the new facility more to attract one of the elite Junior A teams to the small city than to serve the high school program, but the new building helped all the programs in the community.

Back in his home-town high school, Jacques taught physical education and served as the assistant varsity hockey coach and head junior varsity hockey coach. His boss, head coach Tom Galligher, was a man in his early sixties who had been coaching the high school team with indifferent success for more than twenty-five years. He remembered "Jack," all right. Jack was the guy who'd skipped town and probably cost Tom his only chance at a championship. The relationship was off to a bad start.

For the next three years, Jacques suffered in silence as Tom's assistant. Galligher's coaching style was totally opposite from what Jacques had experienced in the Juniors and in college. Galligher had a rigid system and tried to force talent to play the system rather than fit the system to the players' skills. He would yell and threaten his players and had the reputation of, as he himself put it, "kicking a little butt to get these kids to listen up." Jacques knew even at his young age that an inflexible system and coaching by intimidation was not how he wanted to coach. With his JV teams, Jacques did it his own way.

In Jacques' second year at the school, his junior varsity team won their league championship while the varsity had a sub-.500 season—again. In his third year as a varsity assistant, the JVs again excelled, and the varsity team again played mediocre hockey. During the season, Jacques was asked to breakfast by Wilson Morris, a member of the school board and the chief sponsor of the city's Junior team.

"Jack," Morris began, "you seem to be a hell of a coach with your own team. How come your players either quit or don't do squat when they get to the varsity?"

"Mr. Morris, that is a loaded question. There is no way I can answer it in the present circumstances."

"You are as savvy as I thought," Morris responded. "Let me tell you how it is. You don't have to say a thing. I know you came back because you like the town and are well known here. I also know you didn't come back to be an assistant to a dinosaur forever."

Jacques wanted to say something but kept silent.

"Tom Galligher turns sixty-two next month. He has thirty years with the district. We're going to give him a choice of early retirement or hanging around teaching something or other for the next three years. Either way, this is his last year coaching. You want the job?"

Somehow, Jacques knew Morris was not looking for a defense of Galligher or some other phony display of loyalty. "Yes, Mr. Morris, I want the job," was all he said.

Word of Jacques' advancement moved around the small city immediately. Tom Galligher accepted the early retirement offer and immediately quit as coach. He left town quickly and settled in a trailer park in Florida. Jacques took over a 2–11–1 team midseason. He knew he couldn't change the system, but he could change the way the players were treated. He called a meeting with the elected captain and two assistant captains at his house and asked for their input on how to make the team better. The astonished players were at first reluctant to say anything, but all had played for Jacques before and knew he would be straight with them. They offered several suggestions, but, more importantly, afterwards they began to spread the word that Mr. Bottiglier was going to coach the varsity the same way he had the JV players. The team finished with a record of 10–13–3—not great overall record, but a tremendous improvement from midseason.

Bottiglier never had to battle for acceptance with his team or his community. He was clearly a superior coach, and the results showed it. Even though he had a limited pool of players in the small town to draw from, his squad went 15–9–4 the following year and made the playoffs for the first time in a decade. In the subsequent decade, Jacques' teams never missed the playoffs, and in his eighth year as head coach, his team—from the school with the smallest enrollment in the tournament—won the state championship. Jacques had become a beloved institution in his home town.

Just before the beginning of his tenth season, Jacques got a telephone call from his old mentor, Mike Andersen, a call that would change his life. "Jacques, are you stuck on staying in your home town for the rest of your life?"

"Well, Mike," Jacques replied, "it wouldn't take dynamite to get me to move, but I've got a good situation here. I have tenure and no hassles from the athletic director or the board. I'm comfortable with the program and the kids. The only thing I regret is that we just are so damn small. There just aren't that many kids to draw from. Some of the best still opt for the Juniors."

Andersen got to the point of the call. "You know I'm from the Upper Midwest. I played for Paul Bromley, one of the real super high school coaches when he was just starting out. What he has built is extraordinary. Big player base, fantastic support from the community and the boosters, and great facilities. East High is one of the premiere programs in the country. Well, Paul called me the other day to tell me he was going to retire. Apparently the board has appointed a committee to pick his successor, and he wanted to know if I had anyone I'd recommend. I thought of you right away but didn't tell him. Wanted to check it out with you first."

"I'm flattered you would think of me, Mike. I know that program. Heck, they have put a bunch of people into Division I and the pros. I would be nuts not to at least take a look. Thanks." He wrote a letter to the search committee and indicated his interest in the program. Shortly thereafter he received a phone call inviting him to fly in for an interview at the expense of the committee.

Jacques agreed to meet with the committee at the end of the hockey season. During the meeting, Bottiglier was blunt. "I like everything I've seen. You have a first class program, wonderful facilities, and a budget several times what I work with now. I want the job. But you need to know that, while I admire what Paul Bromley has accomplished, I'm not his clone. I need your assurance that I can run the program my way within the constraints of the rules of your league and program mission statement."

After much deliberation, the committee narrowed its search to two candidates: Jacques and Al Wilkinson, the long-time assistant to Bromley. In the end, they chose to offer the standard one-year contract to Jacques. He accepted.

Before he could even move to his new community there was trouble. The local newspaper ran an editorial denouncing the committee's choice of a "foreigner" over "a man who has proved his loyalty to our program for many years." As soon as Jacques heard about the article, he called the man who wrote it. "Just checking, but why did you call me a foreigner?"

The editor, Ed Newton, was nonplused. "Well, heck, Bottiglier, that was a lousy choice of words. What I meant was that you aren't from this area. We thought Al deserved the job. If I offended over the word, I apologize."

"No problem," Jacques replied, "and no apology necessary. I just wanted to see if your maps showed the same Canadian border ours in Vermont do."

"Yeah, they do. And I know you have a good reputation as a coach, Mr. Bottiglier. It's just that Al has a special place at East. I thought he deserved a shot at running the program. I want you to know that Al called me and gave me more hell over the story than you did. He didn't come whining to me when he didn't get the job."

"I appreciate knowing that, sir. All I ask of you and everyone is that they don't pass judgment on the replacement for a legend at least until he gets to town."

"Okay, Jacques," the editor laughed, "you have made me a neutral observer, at least until you lose your first game."

On that bit of gallows humor, the conversation ended, and Jacques let out a sigh. "This isn't going to be the same as taking over for Tom Galligher," he thought. "I either need to do things exactly as they always have been or put my imprint on the program immediately."

Within a few days of moving to his new city, Jacques had a visit from a delegation of youth hockey coaches in the East district. "We just wanted to meet you and welcome you," one said, "and ask you how you want us to plan our programs. If you're going to make a lot of changes, we need to know it."

"Gentlemen, I appreciate the welcome. I don't know what the specific rules are in this state, but in Vermont, the high school and Junior coaches were not permitted to mandate a system for the youth teams in the community."

"Can't here, either," said the spokesman. "It's just that with Paul Bromley, we knew what the kids were going to be expected to do at the high school level, and we put in simplified versions of the same system. Paul didn't do anything against the rules. We don't expect you to, either."

"Glad to hear that," said Jacques. "If you want to know what kind of hockey my teams play, there are plenty of tapes available. Public TV in

Vermont did a whole series on the program after we won the state title. That's about all the leads I can give you until I assess what the team's strengths will be this year. Then you'll see what system we play."

Jacques' next move was to call Al Wilkinson. They agreed to meet at Al's home the next afternoon. Surprising to both of them, they hit it off from the beginning. "Jacques," Al said right up front, "I would be a liar if I told you I wasn't disappointed when I didn't get the job. But I didn't plant that foreigner crap, and I won't do anything to hurt the continued success of East hockey."

"Al, thanks for your candor. I know already you aren't the type to take your disappointment public. You say you want to continue East's tradition of success. So do I. I'd like you to reconsider that letter of resignation you sent to the athletic director. I'd like you to remain as my assistant. You continue to play it straight with me, and we will get along very well."

Wilkinson asked for and received some time to think it over. A few days later, he called Jacques and agreed to remain as an assistant. "Step two complete," thought Jacques.

For the next two months, Al and Jacques studied the program from top to bottom. They watched hundreds of hours of video and did a detailed breakdown of the returning players and those who were expected to compete for the remaining slots. Al proved invaluable in his analysis of the top teams in the state. He knew every coach and how they operated. The information was priceless, and Jacques let Al know how much he appreciated it.

The first day of fall practice, Jacques was more nervous than he had been since his first game as a Junior. He arrived at the arena early, strapped on his skates, and did more than his usual exercises. He then dropped a box of pucks on the ice and proceeded to do shot drills until he felt his arms would fall off. The jitters were exorcised.

In Vermont, Jacques had been lucky to get twenty-five people out for varsity tryouts. Here at East over sixty kids showed up for that first session. Fourteen of them were returning lettermen from Bromley's last squad, which had come within one goal of giving their coach another state championship as a retirement present. In addition, twenty other players had legitimate shots at making the varsity, based on their performance on the sophomore, JV, and community bantam programs. Then there were the unknowns. "One thing for sure," Jacques said to Al, "we won't have to drag the river for players."

Jacques skated to center ice and blew his whistle. The players gathered in front of him. "Gentlemen," he began, "I am proud to be associated with the great program and great tradition that is East High hockey. From what I've seen on tape and from what coach Wilkinson has told me, we have the makings of another fine team. I look forward to the season. Okay, stretches. Captain and assistants take over."

Brent Lund, the captain, had met Jacques several times but had not discussed much in detail with him because of league rules. Now his jaw dropped. He skated over to Jacques. "Mr. Bottiglier, Coach Bromley always led the stretches, what do you want us to do?"

"I've looked over your warm-up program, Captain Lund, and I see no reason to change anything right now. This is your third year on the team, you ought to know the drill by heart. Besides," Jacques grinned, "I've already done my exercises!"

Lund quickly spoke to his two assistant captains, and, after a moment, warm-ups progressed. Al skated over to Jacques. "I see the 'same but different' tactic is having an effect."

"There isn't a whole lot of variety in the basics of conditioning; we both know that. Keeping to the same routine will help get things going quickly. Why screw with something that works? I don't believe in changing things just for the sake of change."

The first few practices were really a weeding-out process. At the end of the first week, Jacques had a pretty good idea of who could skate, check, and shoot. He and Al made the first cuts of the players who obviously lacked basic hockey skills. That left thirty-eight players to compete for twenty-three slots.

The second week came as more of a shock to the veteran players than the newcomers. Paul Bromley had always emphasized a wide-open, rush-the-puck-up-the-ice style, a style that had produced champions when skillful players were abundant but had been less successful when the talent was thinner. From what Jacques had seen, this squad had a great senior goalie, a junior who would push him, two excellent defensive duos, and only one speed line. Jacques had decided during his preseason research to pursue a strong checking style and rely on hard team play and good defense. He didn't think he had the horses to run four lines at high speed for forty-five minutes.

At the end of that week, Brent Lund and one of the assistant captains came to see Jacques after practice. "Mr. Bottiglier," Lund began, "we don't get what you're doing. We all know the system East has always used. We started learning it as little kids. We don't think it should be changed. Coach Bromley always had us work with fixed plays, and you have us working general areas and improvising more. We can't pick all that up so quickly, and the first game is just ten days away."

"Brent, first, I respect what Coach Bromley built and have no intention of tearing the program down. But I am not Paul Bromley, and I do not do things exactly as he did. I teach zone play and good communication because it is the way I think we can best adapt to the players we have. I know it is a change. I know it puts more responsibility on the kids on the ice. That's the way I teach and coach the game. Thank you for coming and giving me your input. Please see me any time you have a question or an idea. The team needs your leadership out there."

Lund and his friend left quietly. Jacques continued to develop what he called "smart hockey." Hard checking and heads-up play were the order of the day. The goalies loved it. They could see their goals-against average going down, and that would help them with the scouts and college recruiters. The other veterans were split. For the first time, some of the players openly complained to their parents about how Mr. Bottiglier was "messing with the system."

One evening, Jacques got a call at home from Ed Newton, the newspaper sports editor who had written the negative editorial about Jacques' hiring. "Just thought you ought to know, Jacques, that a couple of the hockey dads, the ones with more time and money than smarts, are already out to get you. Seems you aren't treating the system with respect, or something like that. Any comment?"

"Not on the record, Ed, but thanks."

"How about off the record?"

"Only this. Go back to what I said to the selection committee when they offered me the job. The minutes of that meeting are public record. And Ed, merci beaucoup."

"You're never going to let me off the hook on that one are you, Jacques? Good night."

The following Monday morning, Brent Lund's father called Jacques. Mark Lund was a successful attorney in the area, had himself played for Paul Bromley, and was the president of the hockey booster club. He was used to getting his way. The conversation started out with a request for Jacques to return to the style of hockey the kids were familiar with. Jacques patiently explained why he wouldn't do that, and the conversation degenerated into threats by Lund, Sr., to "pull half your squad out from under you and see how you take that." Lund, Jr., was not at practice that afternoon.

Brent returned to practice Tuesday but was a poor excuse for a leader on the ice. He dogged it throughout the workout and afterward was pulled aside by Jacques. "Why were you absent yesterday, Brent?" the coach asked.

"I just didn't feel up to it. It's not as much fun anymore."

"Well, Brent, I can't have a team captain showing up when he pleases and sleepwalking through the drills when he does come back. I'm going to suspend you as captain for a while and let you think about what you want to do."

"You can't do that!" Lund exploded. "You didn't make me captain, the guys elected me."

Jacques quietly said, "I can because I'm the coach. I need student leaders who will give the program a chance, not cut it down. As I said, think about things, Brent."

The next day, Brent Lund and four other senior lettermen left the team and signed up to play for a local Junior squad. Before practice, Al sought out Jacques. "I may have made a bit more trouble for us, Jacques," he began. "Brent's father and two other members of the boosters came up to me on the street as I was walking home. They wanted my support in forcing you to change the way you run the program. I'm afraid I used some pretty foul language when I told them where to get off."

Jacques continued to manage his program in a calm manner. He moved several lines around and made plans to keep several young players who previously had not been likely to make the final cut. The new captain, Will Pollard, was the senior goalie and a real quiet leader. The new assistant was a junior winger and a holler guy who kept everyone loose. Practices became more harmonious. Still, several of the veteran players didn't seem to be getting the message. A few days before final cuts were due, Jacques called one senior and four juniors to his office.

"Guys, what's the beef? The other players are coming together as a team and making real progress at learning some new things. You five are just going through the motions."

The players just mumbled some excuses that had nothing to do with the real problem—all were buddies of Brent Lund or hung around with the others who had quit but weren't good enough to play on the Junior team. They were torn between wanting to play the game and annoyance at Bottiglier and the new system.

"I said I would be straight with you and here's where I stand," Jacques said. "You have to make your own decisions. I'm not going to change the way I coach. Brent and his friends aren't coming back. Right now, none of you are hustling enough to make the final cut. I tell you that, not as a threat, just as information. You have three practices to shape it up."

During those final practices, it was obvious to Jacques and Al that two of the kids had been shaken out of their funk by the blunt words from the coach. Both made the team. The senior and two of the juniors were cut from the varsity. The juniors were assigned to the JV, and the senior was told of opportunities for play in the community program. All were stunned.

Once again, several members of the booster club, led by Mark Lund, made their anti-Jacques feelings known—not just to the coaches but formally in a letter to the athletic director with a copy to the newspaper. The A.D. refused to take any action against the coach, and the newspaper ignored the copy sent to them.

The first game came. It would have been easier for Jacques if it had been against a weak opponent, but this was the famous season-opening "Skate East" tourney hosted by East High and featuring eight top schools from a three-state area. Jacques' team went down to another hard checking squad from a neighboring state 2–1. The coach was pleased with the effort his now very young team had put forth and told them so after the game. The next game was Jacques first victory at East, 1–0, as his goalie/captain made thirty-eight saves, including stopping a breakaway in the last minute. The team lost the final game of the tournament 4–1 to the previous year's state champion.

With nine of the fourteen lettermen he had counted on off the team, Jacques was happy to survive the tournament with a win and get on with the season ahead of him. The team improved as time passed, but it certainly was not winning with the regularity of the usual East juggernaut. During a Christmas tournament, the senior goalie broke his leg in a pileup around the crease and was out for the year. The young man showed up at practice the first day after surgery and became almost another assistant coach for the balance of the year. Most of his time was spent working with the sophomore goalie who had been called up from JV.

Halfway through the tough league season, East stood 10–7–2, with only four league games. The grumbling in the community started again. This time, no player was involved. Mark Lund appeared before a school board meeting and demanded that an investigation be launched into the "verbal intimidation and threats" used by coach Bottiglier in "forcing players who had done nothing wrong to leave the team." The board tabled the request and referred the matter to the athletic director. The A.D. knew exactly what was going on—knew that Jacques never threatened or abused anyone and, in fact, was earning the respect of every kid who played for him. He wrote back to the board that he could find no evidence to support Lund's allegations and would take no action.

That incident marked the high tide of opposition to Jacques from parents and others in the community, although Jacques still had to fight the occasional skirmish in his battle to control his program and his methods. The team continued to play good tight-checking hockey. The youngsters Jacques had promoted to the varsity ahead of their time began to make significant contributions. East finished third in its league that season and made it to the state sectional tournament as the fourth seed. They won the first round against a veteran, high-scoring team but lost in overtime in the semifinals 1–0.

The early exit from the tournament started some of the more rabid hockey fans in the district muttering, but the parents of the team members were largely silent. The newspaper came out with an editorial just after East had been knocked out of postseason play and commended the players and the coaching staff for making the best of a rocky transition year.

At the hockey awards banquet, Will Pollard, the injured goalie, was voted by his peers as most inspirational teammate, even though he played less than half the season. Jacques made sure that Mike Anderson received tapes of Will's previous season as well as games from his aborted senior year. During dinner, Will announced that he had accepted an academic scholarship to attend college at Anderson's university and to play for the coach if his leg held up.

Then he had the other members of the varsity gather around as he presented a large, elegantly wrapped package to Jacques and a similar one to Al. Inside, each coach found a small box packaged within the large one. Both coaches opened their small box and looked at the contents in puzzlement. Jacques had a tube of instant epoxy glue marked "Part A," and Al had a similar tube marked "Part B." At this point, Will and the one other senior on the team brought out two East High hockey medallions, each neatly sawed in half and invited the two coaches, who could have walked away from each other, to mix up the epoxy and put the medallions back together. When they had done so, Will asked the coaches to look at the reverse of the medallions. The inscription on each was the same: "To Coach Bottiglier and Coach Wilkinson from your team. We all stuck together."

Jacques Bottiglier now has coached at East for three seasons. He hasn't won a state title yet, but this past season his team came close. The school board that had voted 5–2 to renew his first contract for one additional year just voted unanimously to offer him a five-year contract.

RICK:

"Essentially this story is about what is called 'the battle for structure.' It happens whenever a new coach comes into a program with a lot of tradition and history and attempts to define his or her position and to make the program his or her own.

"Jacques presents an example of how to battle for structure in a positive way. He has confidence in himself as a person and a coach. He sets the newspaper editor straight, wins over his chief rival for the job, engages the boosters, the parents, and the players—and all the while he's defining his position and letting everyone know how things are going to be.

"Jacques would have been much less successful if he'd ridden into town like the new marshal and refused to bring key people into his system.

"There is a delicate balance at work here. You have to establish the 'I' position, but you can't shut out the world out in the process. You have to get key groups and individuals to buy into your program. Very early in the game, Jacques enlisted the support of Al Wilkinson, the long-time assistant coach who had competed with him for the head coaching job. Jacques validated Al's continuing value to the program. By doing so, he won over Al, and then Al helped in the battle with the broader community.

"Every time you define what it is you want, what you're about as a coach, there is going to be some resistance from some people. That's why I call it a 'battle' for structure. Every interested party, including the kids, will want to control the program to some degree. They want to be in charge. So no matter what action you take, there's going to be a reaction, and often this reaction is disproportionately stronger than the original action you took.

"People feel stress during times of change, and they don't like that. They're going to try to reach a level of comfort again, which usually means returning things to the way they were before they changed. Sometimes it's possible to make a few concessions, but overall you have to be very clear about who is defining what's going on, who's the captain of the ship.

"These battles go on all the time, often in subtle ways, even before the new coach starts the job. If you don't acknowledge these conflicts and deal with them head-on, you can lose the war before you even realize there has been a battle.

"I can't stress this enough: You must win the battle for structure in order to be effective as a coach."

JOHN:

"I almost lost my first battle for structure when I went from assistant coach to head coach. I wasn't much older than some of my players. All of a sudden my relationship with the players changed. I changed some of the ways we did things, and the older players resisted the changes at every turn.

"Halfway through the year our veteran team was barely playing .500 ball, and the media started complaining that I was too young and inexperienced for the job. I didn't see it coming, and it really hurt. Fortunately, two things happened: The guy who hired me stood behind me publicly and privately, and we started winning some games.

"Battles for structure aren't limited to major college athletics. They go on at every level of sports. The new youth-leagues coach who wants to keep a particular age group of girls' soccer as a house league is going to be in a battle with those who want a traveling league. The coach who values teaching fundamentals over winning is certain to be attacked. A new youth-league coach has to be just as aware of the effects of change as does the high school or college coach. If you change something, there will be a reaction. You will be second-guessed; you will be challenged.

"Be prepared for these battles. They happen more frequently when you first take over a position, but, believe me, they are still there even after you've been coaching the same program for twenty years. Any change brings a battle, even if the change occurs within an established program or under an established coach. You need to go in to a situation with a clearly defined set of expectations of what you want to do. Of course, it's preferable to try to justify the changes in advance and rally the support of the players, parents, and community, but sometimes you just have to go ahead with what you think is right for the program."

Ralph: Who Needs This Stuff?

Ralph Morgan is fifty-five years old. He is in his fifteenth season as head men's basketball coach at a major university in a southern state. He has won two national championships for his current school and another at a smaller school. That first win, which was called at the time "a tribute to hustle, dedication, and great coaching," got him the position of prestige he now holds.

Ralph, an African-American, grew up in a middle-class family in the de facto segregated South of the forties and fifties. Ralph's father, a veterinarian, taught him respect for honesty and forthrightness. These traits became his hallmark as a coach and a person. His mother, a track star in high school, gave him his competitive spirit. He was the first black man to earn a full athletic scholarship to his state university. He starred not only on the court but on campus as well. In his senior year, he was captain of the basketball team and the only person of color to serve on the student senate. His ROTC experience won him a commission as an army officer upon graduation.

His four-year army hitch, including a thirteen-month tour of duty in Vietnam, further shaped Ralph's character. Military service honed his leadership skills; the troops under his command considered him to be person of honor and dedication. His stint in Vietnam also engendered in him a hatred of illicit drugs and the damage they could cause.

Ralph always had a desire to teach and, after being mustered out of active service, he returned to his alma mater to work on a master's degree. The new coach of the basketball team knew Ralph and hired him as a graduate assistant coach. The small stipend helped with tuition, but the experience Ralph received was priceless. He later said, "I spent two years with that man and received far more than my master's degree and a few dollars in payment. I got a doctorate in the realities of coaching. I learned the mentoring system firsthand—even though they didn't call it that then. I still think it's the best way to learn. I continue to practice it, although now I am the mentor."

Ralph's mentor couldn't offer him a full-time position, but he did recommend him for an assistant coaching job at a mid-size university in California. Ralph served as an assistant for four years, then assumed the head coaching position upon the retirement of his predecessor. At the age of thirty, he felt fully prepared for the responsibilities he was taking on.

In three years, Ralph rebuilt the program and took his team to the Division II finals. A Division I program noticed him. The school was not much bigger than his present one but with a much more aggressive approach to playing winning basketball. Ralph moved to his new assignment in the Midwest but continued to recruit heavily in the South and West where he was best known. It was at this new school that he won his first Division I, NCAA championship, beating a legendary program and coach. A year later, the legend retired, and Ralph was hired to replace him.

At forty, Ralph was at the top of his profession. He had one of the best programs in the country and could take his pick of outstanding student athletes who wanted to play for him. For the next twelve years, Ralph coached with the same dedication to honesty and straight talk he had displayed all his life. He constantly changed his approach to the game depending on the skills of his players and the best methods and systems of the day. He was very happy in his job and in his life.

Then, one day, Ralph realized that he was becoming less and less satisfied with coaching. He commented to Ann, his wife and partner of thirty years, "I don't know what's wrong. I love the game. When I'm at practice or in a game, it's the same thrill. The administration has been great to us. The facilities are all anyone could ask for. But there is a lot of change going on outside the program that I can't control. That stuff is beginning to grind on me."

Ann and Ralph continued the thread of that conversation over many months. It turned out that what concerned Ralph the most were changes in the personalities and behaviors of the kids he was recruiting and coaching. Following some lean years, when his winning percentage was not up to his or the University's usual high expectations, he had, for the first time, recruited a couple of kids with "baggage"—a history of violent behavior and suspected gang activity but no known drug involvement. He knew the kids had some problems when he signed them, but he felt that he could turn them around. And they were very, very good basketball players.

He and Ann had always tried to make the members of the team feel at home. The kindness, love, and respect they showed had almost always been reciprocated by the players. His personal rapport with the players was one of his strongest motivational tools. With the new recruits, however, there were problems from the start. One guy was caught by university police with crack, and another was arrested by the city police for dealing drugs. The user, Ralph tried to help; the dealer, he kicked off the team. He had seen firsthand what drugs could do to the morale of a unit in Vietnam and had little tolerance for their use and none for their sale.

In the first twenty-five years of his career, only four of Ralph's athletes had had any problems with drugs or alcohol and only five more had had any criminal problems, almost all of a minor nature. In the last three years, though, he had suspended or dismissed eight players for drug use, three others had been caught dealing drugs, and several more had been convicted of such felonies as assault and armed robbery. His "recruits with baggage" helped win a championship but at a terrible cost to the cohesiveness of the team and to Ralph's public image.

The change in the kids was not the only thing grinding on Ralph. For the first time in his career, his program had been investigated and sanctioned by the NCAA for recruiting violations. Ralph discovered the problem himself. An assistant coach had made contacts with high school athletes outside the proper time period and, together with several alumni boosters in town, had gotten jobs for team members in violation of NCAA rules.

Ralph reported the problem to the athletic director. The assistant was terminated, and the university proposed sanctions it hoped would satisfy the NCAA. The investigation by the university and the NCAA took over a year. During the process, the NCAA discovered that Ann had several times given team members a few dollars to carry them over. "They were absolutely destitute," she told the investigator. "Ralph and I have always given the players some home cooking and some loving. Some needed a little more. If $10 helped a young man get his only suit cleaned so he could go to a job interview with pride, then I gave it to him. If a $50 bus ticket let a kid attend his mother's funeral, who wouldn't help if she could? If those are violations, then the rules are wrong!"

Ralph's program was punished with a one-year ban on tournament play and the loss of a scholarship for two years, among other things. Ralph thought about resigning then but felt it would be running out on a problem he was ultimately responsible for.

This past season, the team's performance was lackluster, and—rare for a team coached by Ralph—there were serious morale problems. Ralph had always been able to change himself to meet the needs of his players, the hallmark of a great coach. This season, however, had overwhelmed his capacity for change. Two players who would have stayed with the team another year opted instead for the NBA draft. Ralph really couldn't blame them. Another player ended up in jail for a gang-related shooting during the off-season. The team also lost a prize recruit because the kid's father didn't want him going to a "dirty" program. When Ralph heard those words, he said out loud for the first time to Ann, "I don't need this! My honor is my life. I don't need some son of a bitch who doesn't know anything about the situation calling my program dirty."

Ann was concerned. Ralph just didn't use language like that. Worse, his blood pressure had been rising recently, and he now had to take medication to control it. She hated the thought of her husband dying young from the stress of a job that was no longer was satisfying to either of them. She convinced Ralph to go away for a week, just the two of them, to a small cabin on the coast. They did a lot of walking on the beach and talking about the future. Money wasn't an issue. Ralph had been paid well, and they had invested wisely. Moreover, several television networks had approached Ralph to probe his interest in becoming a commentator. And the Black Coaches Association, which Ralph had helped found, was looking for a paid executive director.

The sticking point for Ralph was that he still loved to coach. He didn't want to give it up completely. But he really had come to hate going to his office every day and wondering what kind of Stuff was going to ambush him this time.

By the end of the week, Ann and Ralph had come to the decision they both knew was right. Ralph Morgan, 508 lifetime wins, four-time Coach of the Year, and three-time NCAA champion, resigned, effective the end of the academic year.

JOHN:

"Unfortunately, Ralph's decision to leave the profession he loves is becoming more and more prevalent. Here is a guy who seems to have done it all right. He had great mentors, paid his dues as an assistant learning the profession, and moved up the head coaching ranks to the very top.

"He adapted and changed with the times and with the types of players he had. He really connected with the kids. His wife provided needed balance in his life and was a full partner in making sure the kids on the team had the best possible total experience. This guy was a rare, rare jewel in the coaching profession.

"And yet The Other Stuff ends up driving him out. What a loss for everyone!

"I wish I had some great wisdom to pass on to other coaches to help them through this type of situation, but I don't. Sometimes you just can't accommodate the rate of change inside the game and out. Some coaches are more resilient and stay through all kinds of problems. Others decide to leave. That doesn't make them better or worse as coaches or as human beings.

"Why does Tom Osborne leave at the peak of his career, and why does Joe Paterno stay on, happy and effective in his seventies? Why does Dean Smith, a legend who really connected with his players, hang it up, and Bob Knight, an equally great coach, hang on and do a superb coaching job during several very tough periods?

"The answers have to be personal; they're certainly not connected with the success of their respective programs.

"About the only advice I can give to a fellow coach is to constantly monitor your situation. Make sure your staff and your players are fully aware of what the mission is and what the rules are.

And most of all, establish open communication with your players, your assistants, and your administration.

"Even if you do all this, though, you can still be disappointed by the off-the-field conduct of your players. You have to remember that you cannot be responsible for the conduct of another person. That person is responsible for his or her own conduct. All you can do is provide a structure, a set of expectations, and a model for the players you coach. And you just have to be ready to accept that that may not be enough."

RICK:

"When stress builds up, it can create a crisis. In Ralph's case, the stress built up over a long period of time. It wasn't the Xs and Os, the pressures of meeting high expectations on the court, that created stress for Ralph. He was a master at meeting those expectations, and thrived on the pressure of competition at the highest level. No, the stresses that brought about Ralph's career crisis had to do with things over which he had little control. Kids change; there's nothing new about that. But some recent changes in societal and juvenile behavior are particularly hard for some people to take. To a person like Ralph, who hated drugs and hated what drugs did to people, the rise in drug use and drug dealing among the population from which some of his best players came was extremely disturbing.

"The NCAA sanctions added to his stress. Ralph was a stickler for complying with the rules, and he blamed himself for not supervising his assistant coach better. In periods of reflection and complete honesty, Ralph knew he could have nipped the situation years earlier if he'd only acted more forcefully.

"The flash point was not when his wife became involved in the investigation. Ralph didn't know about Ann's "petty cash fund" but supported it in spirit and was proud of the way Ann had handled herself during the inquiry. The flash point of the crisis really came when the father of a recruit called Ralph's program "dirty." To a decorated former Army officer and a coach with a deservedly impeccable reputation, honor was a sacred thing. At that point, he crossed the line between staying and leaving.

"The most important thing Ralph had going for him as he worked to resolve his crisis was the strength, intelligence, and love of his wife. Ann had always been a true partner in Ralph's career and acted in unison with him as the final decision was reached.

"Ralph may experience periods of regret for leaving the job he's loved so much, but he's fortunate to have so many opportunities awaiting him, as talented people often do. A phrase I'm fond of in this context is 'transitional objects.' Transitional objects are tangible things one can hold on to during a period of change. A child might have a teddy bear that helps the youngster get through a period of change from complete dependence on a parent to one of more independence. For some coaches, broadcasting sports on television serves as a transitional object. They can still feel connected and a part of the game by helping a television audience understand it better. Becoming a television commentator is, in this case, one of several possible transitional objects available to Ralph to help him fill the void he will surely experience as he withdraws from active coaching.

"Ralph is obviously a fine coach and a superior person. But he is not a saint. When his program started to go a bit downhill, he made a conscious decision to go recruit kids with known problems—

drugs, violence, gang activities. He recruited these kids and won another championship with them. Unfortunately he couldn't reform the kids the way he'd hoped. He forgot that he was running a big-time basketball program, not Boys Town. Perhaps he thought that winning another championship would allow him to recruit the type of kids he really wanted—top athletes without any personal baggage. But Ralph was taking an obvious risk, and, in the end, his choices came back to burn him.

"Ralph had plenty of good reasons to leave when he did. That should be the message for all coaches. Make sure that, if you are thinking about leaving the coaching ranks, you are doing so for the right reasons. Make sure that it's what you want to do, when you want to do it. The decision is not going to be the same for everyone. If you really love to teach, if you really love being around kids, then, unlike Ralph, you might have chosen to stay in the game, to go back and recruit kids with lesser talent but fewer off-court problems, and to settle for winning fewer games.

"But if you had other opportunities awaiting you outside of coaching and if, like Ralph, you found that The Other Stuff had taken all the joy out of coaching, then the best thing to do might be just to walk away from the game. Ralph had had enough. He left the game for reasons that were right for him. He wasn't the loser; the sport was."

Section Two

Relationships

There is No "Right" Way

In the last section, we discussed the "I" of coaching—knowing yourself, being your own person, making your own decisions. Knowing yourself, we argued, is the first step on the path to successful coaching.

Now, we'd like to look outward at some of the important relationships in a coach's life—relationships with a spouse or significant other, with children and other family members, with colleagues, and with players—and examine how coaching affects and is affected by these relationships.

We'll begin with the most obvious relationship: that between a coach and a player. This relationship varies widely, from very little direct contact to intense personal involvement. Either extreme may be appropriate depending on such factors as the size of the program, the type of sport, the age of the athlete, the assigned duties of the coach, and so on.

For example, the head coach of a major college football program may have little direct contact with his players. The sheer number of players on the team dictates that the head coach delegate much of the relationship building to the assistant coaches. An offensive lineman might have a close relationship with his position coach, strength coach, academic advisor, or trainer, but rarely with the head man.

At the other end of the scale is the coach of an individual in a sport such as gymnastics, tennis, golf, or diving. Here the relationship is more direct and personal. Many coaches in these sports function as de facto parents to the athlete, sometimes going so far as to take the young player into the coach's home to live as a member of his or her family.

Of course, not every football coach remains aloof from his players and not every individual coach becomes a surrogate parent. There is a broad range of acceptable relationships between coaches and players in every sport.

Pushing the Envelope

All of us can cite examples of coaches at every level in every sport who succeed while operating right at the edge of acceptable conduct. You've seen successful coaches, even in youth sports, who verbally intimidate players to control them and who will try to motivate by "getting in the face" of a player. You know of coaches who believe that rigorous physical conditioning will overcome a lot of problems and who will work their players to the point of collapse to build stamina and strength. You also have watched the coach who uses a pseudoparental relationship with players to influence them, thereby boosting performance and increasing wins.

It is not our aim here to argue for one style or method of motivation and teaching over another. It's up to you to decide what works with your personality, and in a given situation. Intimidation, control, nurturing— each has produced champions; each has made coaches successful. Each has also resulted in failure when applied inappropriately.

How, then, can you determine what type of relationship with a player is appropriate?

You are Their Coach, Not Their Parent, Therapist, or Lover!

The vast majority of us who coach think we can and will make a difference in the lives of our players. We look at the lessons we learned from participation in sports and want younger players to have similar, positive experiences. In other words, we care about the people we coach.

We are absolutely right to care. Caring is a normal, healthy human emotion and is a great motivator for coaches and players alike. Caring for other people is good.

The first thing we need recognize, though, is that a line exists between coach and player. A coach plays many roles, so it is easy for us to inadvertently confuse some of these roles. But we have to be very careful when we begin to cross the line between being the player's coach and being his or her parent, therapist, or lover. Crossing this line is fraught with danger to the coach, to the player, and to those close to each of them.

While assuming the role of coach-parent may draw a higher level of performance from an athlete, it can also create an unhealthy dependency. Likewise, many coaches can and do function well as a social therapist to their players, but few if any have the proper training and skills to act as a professional therapist. (We'll explain more about the distinction between social therapist and professional therapist later.) It is dangerous for a layperson to pretend to be a psychologist or psychiatrist. Both player and coach can be damaged in the process.

Even more dangerous is romantic involvement with a player. A coach who has an affair with a player, whether it is sexual or emotional, risks not only his or her job and career but other personal relationships as well. Most athletic programs have policies against sexual relationships between coaches and players. Many explicitly define a relationship with someone over whom you have power as sexual harassment. Depending on the difference in age between the player and coach, there could be criminal implications as well.

JOHN:

"It's easy for a new coach to become too involved with his or her players. Most coaches are people-oriented to begin with. When we start out, either as volunteers or as assistant coaches, we are very close to the athletes. In a community program, we might even be coaching our own child. An assistant coach in a large university program is going to do a lot of the recruiting and will probably bond with the kids more quickly than the head coach.

"Sometimes a coach who has been hurt by being too close to a player will go overboard in the opposite direction and become bitter, resentful, and cynical—a coach who withdraws from any emotional contact with players.

"Both types will be less effective than the coach who strikes a balance in his or her relationships with players.

"In particular, you have to be careful that you don't become so involved with your players that you harm your relationships with the people you really love and value—your family and friends. When you bury yourself in coaching, you risk separation, divorce—the breakup of your family. A good coach understands these risks and deals with them in a manner that meets his or her life objectives, not just his or her short-term coaching goals.

"In my twenty-plus years in the profession, I've seen many coaches cross the line. A few of them, primarily those with good mentors, managed to step back and get on with their careers. Most, however, left coaching—either they quit or were fired. And many lost a lot more than just their jobs.

"As coaches, we need to connect with our players. We have to be willing to take risks. But we also have to be sure that the rewards justify the risks."

RICK:

"It's true. Good coaching is a risky business. In order to realize the rewards of coaching, you have to be willing to risk interacting with your players.

"What we want to do now is to offer you three examples of coaches who had strong personal relationships with their players. You may think of these as cautionary tales in that they illustrate what can go wrong when you interact closely with a player. They also illustrate the value of having someone you can rely on to help you through a tough situation—a mentor or social therapist—because, unfortunately, a lot of what coaches need to know about these types of real-life situations aren't taught in coaching courses."

An Emotional Affair —Alex Crosses the Line

Alexander Dowdell is the thirty-eight-year-old former coach of a major Division I women's volleyball program. He was a very good player at one of the West Coast schools that always seemed to be at the top in the men's sport, and was one of the last players cut from the national team, which went on to win two world championships in the mid-eighties.

After his playing days ended, Alex turned his considerable passion and energy to coaching, beginning as an assistant coach of a men's team at a small college. He switched to the women's game when the opportunity arose to become head coach at a California high school known for its volleyball program and for the number of players going on to Division I teams.

After honing his skills at the high school level for three years, Alex was named head women's volleyball coach at the same small college where he had started his coaching career. He won several championships for the college, developing a reputation for being a caring coach who always had time for his players. Many described his style as "both coach and substitute parent."

In his first year as head coach at the college, Alex met Sarah Hildingson, a junior on his team. Alex got to know Sarah as an intelligent and beautiful young woman. They often met privately and talked about Sarah's personal life—not just volleyball. By the end of Sarah's final season, an emotional relationship had developed between them. After graduating, Sarah was reluctant to accept a job offer in a distant city, but both Alex and Sarah agreed that some time away from each other would help them gain perspective on their relationship. Sarah accepted the job and became an analyst with an insurance company.

Their long-distance relationship not only continued, but blossomed into a courtship. They called each other every day and visited each other whenever their schedules permitted. Eventually, they became lovers. A year later, Alex was offered the head coaching job at an eastern university that was committed to upgrading its program. He accepted the offer—not only was it a major step up for him, but he now would be only an hour from Sarah.

Alex proposed almost immediately, and the couple married over the Christmas break—the only time of the year when Alex wasn't either recruiting, conducting practices, or coaching games. Sarah commented, "I'm learning early what the wife of a coach has to go through. Just think— a four-day honeymoon squeezed in between practice and a recruiting visit. I'm glad I played for you. At least I have some clue about your life."

A year later, son Geoffrey was born, followed two years later by daughter Samantha. By this time, Alex was making enough money with his coaching, clinics, summer camp, and local radio contract that Sarah could quit her job and become a stay-at-home mother. Things couldn't have been better.

When Geoff was three and Sam was one, Alex was named head coach at one of the premier women's programs in the country. Sarah was proud of her husband's success and moved her family across the country with great anticipation.

At his new university, it was not uncommon for crowds of twelve thousand or more to pack the field house to see his team play. Alex's coaching style remained the same. He continued to involve himself intimately in the lives of his players, counseling them on personal as well sport-related issues and motivating them with nurturing, friendly, and supportive techniques. Alex not only maintained the winning tradition of the program, in his third year his team won a national championship. He recruited the top players from all over the country and even had two players with national team experience in other countries.

But while Alex's coaching life was going well, his family relationships were deteriorating. Sarah confided in a friend that she was jealous of Alex's relationships with his players. "He spends far more time with his girls than with us. The kids and I are just there. He comes home at night, and we go to bed. He rarely is home early enough even to tuck the kids in, let alone play with them. Frankly, even when we are in bed, he isn't the lover he used to be."

The friend was not much help. She told Sarah it was "well known" that the women's volleyball team was "the most promiscuous group on campus." Sarah remembered the intimate relationship she had shared with Alex when she played for him. He had made her feel very special, and she knew he had continued that style of coaching. She began to brood about the possibility that her husband was having an affair with one or more of his players. One thing she knew for sure: Things couldn't continue the way they were.

A couple of weeks later when Alex was actually home on a Sunday afternoon, Sarah sent the kids to a neighbor and confronted Alex. She told him how she felt about him excluding his family from his life, putting his players before his wife and kids. And how sick and tired she was of being "in second place to whichever of your girls you are screwing this year. And don't try to deny it."

Alex had listened to the tirade silently but with increasing agitation. When Sarah accused him of infidelity, he blew up. "I am not sleeping with any of my players. I never crossed that line, not even with you. If you think about it, you know what I'm telling you is true."

Sarah retorted, "You know, Alex, even if you're not sleeping with them, you might as well be. You have your one-on-one time with the players, your private meetings. Having sex with them? I don't know, but you sure are doing everything else. In case you've forgotten, you aren't married to your team. You're married to me.

"And while we're on the subject of family, you are Geoff and Samantha's father, not your players' father. I'm sure the kids would love to have just a tiny fraction of the time you spend with the team."

The Sunday blowup between Sarah and Alex did nothing to clear the air. Sarah continued with her suspicions that Alex was being unfaithful; Alex continued to deny he was having a sexual liaison with a player. Sarah moved out and took the children with her to an apartment in a nearby city. Alex was upset; Sarah, he felt, was being unjust and unreasonable. He loved Sarah—he loved coaching. And now it looked like he was going to have to choose between them.

Then something happened to bring the situation to a head: A player walked in on Alex and Wendy Miller, the team captain. They were cuddling together on a couch, being quite intimate. The team had been whispering suspiciously about the special relationship between coach and captain, but this was too much. The player reported the incident to Joe Merden, the athletic director, who called Alex on the carpet.

"Alex, you are a fine coach. Your teams make this university proud. But I think you've gone over the line between being a coach and being something else with your players. We have rules here about coaches and faculty fraternizing with students in a sexual manner. Even if it was consensual, you are leaving the university, this department, and yourself wide open to a charge of sexual harassment. You know very well that a young person is vulnerable to any suggestion of someone with power over them. You've been to the seminars. You know the rules."

"But Joe," Alex said, "we weren't having sex. I was comforting her because she was having a bad time with a family problem, and, to be honest, she was sympathetic to my family problems. It's all over campus that Sarah left me."

"It doesn't matter, Alex, whether you technically had sex with her. You two were in a compromising position, and you got caught. I have to do something about this. I also want to help you and Sarah with your problems if possible. I like and respect both of you."

"Joe, when Sarah hears about this, she will file for divorce for sure. I can't let that happen. I love her and the kids. I have never been unfaithful to her."

The athletic director was silent for what seemed to Alex to be forever. Then he said, "Alex, you are suspended from your position for one month for conduct in violation of the rules of this department and of your contract with the university. You will have no contact with the team, the assistant coaches, or any individual on the team. During that period, I want you to talk to a psychologist I know who has worked on a private basis with some other people in similar positions. At the end of the month, we'll talk again."

Alex Dowdell had just gone from winning a national championship to being suspended for inappropriate conduct with a player. Both his career and his marriage were on very thin ice. He was devastated. He considered resigning and applying for a coaching assignment overseas. He had made some contacts in Europe when he'd coached a junior national squad there the year before. He certainly didn't want to spill his guts to any shrink. He had never felt comfortable with the idea of getting counseling and questioned now how it could possibly help his situation. Then he thought about his wife and kids. He had to support them and couldn't afford to get fired for refusing a condition of his suspension. With a sigh, he picked up the phone and make an appointment to see Dr. Paul Hoch, who agreed to meet him early the next morning.

Paul Hoch was not at all what Alex expected. He was the antithesis of the stereotypical shrink. Paul was an athlete who swam in national competitions even though he was over fifty. He had coached swimming and diving in the past and still helped out with his community program even though his schedule of patients and consulting would have tested the stamina of a much younger man. After a few minutes of small talk, Alex thought to himself, "Well, at least the guy isn't someone who doesn't know squat about athletics and coaching. Maybe he can help me sort things out."

The hardest thing Alex had to do after several sessions with Dr. Hoch was to call Sarah and ask that she and, eventually, the children, join him in counseling. He actually broke down on the phone. Sarah's response surprised him. She agreed to come to the next session. She told Paul Hoch, "If I had suggested to Alex that we get counseling, he never would have agreed. So, in a way, I'm glad he got caught with that player."

Alex's suspension was lifted after a month, and he rejoined his team. Several things had changed in his absence. The players no longer looked to Alex as a substitute parent and father confessor. That bond had been broken. The other change had occurred in Alex himself. He was beginning to see that he could be a good husband and father as well as a good coach.

It wasn't easy. Alex, Sarah, Geoff, and even little Samantha saw Dr. Hoch over a period of almost a year. What started as individual counseling turned into family therapy. Gradually, Sarah began to realize that she could share some of Alex's coaching life and provide the emotional support that maybe he had been looking for from his players. Between Paul Hoch and the athletic director, Alex learned the basics of changing from being a coach-manipulator, who won by being emotionally close to his players, to being a coach-facilitator, who cared for his players but put family relationships first.

The struggle goes on to this day. The university did not renew Alex's contract. He has found a temporary position as coach of a European national team. He and Sarah still have problems, but at least they are talking about them. The family moved to the European capital where Alex now works. Without the recruiting pressures, Alex is spending more time with his children and with Sarah. Nothing is the same. No one in the family is completely comfortable with the situation, but at least Alex has learned that it's dangerous to become too emotionally involved with his players. He now knows that the problem with walking so close to this line is that sometimes you don't know, or don't care, when you've crossed it.

JOHN:

"I think this story really highlights how easy it is, as a coach, to get emotionally involved with players.

"Number one, because you're around them so much, you have a tendency to feel that you are more responsible for them than you actually are or should be.

"Number two, you want to fix all of a player's problems so that he or she can perform without distractions on the field. In this case, I'm not so sure whether the motivation is to help the kid or win more games. Probably a little of both.

"Often, when we recruit kids, we tell them that the team is a family whose members care about and support one another, and from the beginning we naturally tend to treat players as members of

---

a family. But this sort of bonding puts us very close to a line that we probably don't want to cross.

"During my career, I've seen several situations similar to the one Alex was in. In almost every case, the coach was controlling and emotionally manipulative. I'm not saying that such a coaching style is always wrong. There have been successful coaches in every sport who controlled their players tightly—rarely letting players make their own decisions, have free time, or interact with people outside the program. Institutions will support this type of coach if he or she can fill the stands and persuade alumni to make large donations. They will support this type of coach—to a point.

"The more you intrude on your player's life, the more likely you are to trap yourself the way Alex did. Players don't want to disappoint their coach and will do nearly anything to please him or her. Becoming intimately involved with players is playing with dynamite. It can cost you your job. It can cost you your family."

RICK:

"Only when everything is collapsing around him does Alex even have a clue that what he has done might be over the line. Until he is suspended from his job and threatened with divorce, he refuses to believe that he has a problem.

"Alex doesn't think he's done anything wrong because he hasn't physically consummated a relationship with a player, but he might just as well have. He has been conducting intimate, emotional relationships with people under his control. Whether he has had actual sex with any of them is really not important.

"By some standards, Alex is guilty of sexual harassment: He has had intimate relations with someone over whom he has considerable authority. When one person has power over another, as in this case, consent becomes problematic. The following is the policy statement of a major university: 'Consenting romantic and sexual relationships between staff and students, while not expressly forbidden, are generally deemed very unwise.' In other words, the burden of proof to demonstrate consent is going to be on the staff member, not on the student. And how can a person in authority really know if an inferior is consenting freely or out of fear? Even if consent weren't an issue, the perceived objectivity and fairness of the person in authority would be. Alex's players reacted angrily when they caught him in a compromising position with the team captain. Ironically, his persona as a caring and concerned friend that he had so carefully nurtured over the years was destroyed in that single moment.

"Alex often rationalized his behavior by claiming, 'I didn't have sex with her.' That's not the point. The point is that his players took the place of his wife and children in fulfilling his emotional needs. If Alex continues to do this sort of thing, he is going to lose his family. His only hope, if he wants to stay in the game, is to act more as a coach-facilitator than a coach-manipulator.

"Acting as a coach-manipulator carries risks for all those involved. This style of coaching requires the athlete to become emotionally dependent on the coach. The athlete is motivated out of a desire to please, or at least to avoid disappointing, the coach. Some coaches are masters at exploiting this sort of relationship to get what they want out of an athlete. The relationship works for the athlete as long as he or she is able to satisfy the coach's demands. Problems arise, however, when the athlete fails in this function. The more attached the athlete is to the coach, the more profound is his or her disappointment, and the keener the sense of failure.

"The coach-manipulator risks crossing professional boundaries (or appearing to cross them, which can be just as bad), the consequences of which can range from loss of credibility with players to legal liability. Teaching athletes to be dependent leaves coaches with no one to blame but themselves when the athletes makes poor decisions.

"Rather than teaching dependency, the coach-facilitator teaches responsibility. Assuming the role of consultant or expert advisor, the coach-facilitator tries to help players think critically and independently."

Marty is Thrown a Curve

Marty Stern works long hours. He recently was made a partner of his law firm in the city twenty miles from his suburban home. Marty and his wife Lenore encourage their kids to play sports both for fun and for the values they feel come from team competition. Lenore even took a turn coaching an intracommunity soccer team when their daughter showed an interest in the sport. Marty had played baseball in high school and college and was a good enough pitcher to get a quick look from the pros. He never played pro ball, but he has kept up with the game and still enjoys playing in an "over thirty-five" league.

When the Stern's son Mike was selected to pitch on their community "A" traveling baseball team for thirteen-year-olds, Marty was overjoyed. Mike was just developing physically but had good control, a better-than-average fastball, and solid instincts for the game. A month before preseason practice started, the long-time coach of the traveling team suffered a heart attack and the community athletic board asked Marty to coach the team.

Marty was flattered and excited, especially at the prospect of coaching Mike. The first thing he did was to have a talk with Jack Wilson, the chairman of the community's Youth Athletic Association. "Jack, I read over the rules of this traveling league we're going to be in, and they don't say anything about throwing curves. I think thirteen is just too young to be putting that kind of stress on a developing arm. At this age kids should be taught the fundamentals of the pitching motion and how to get the ball over the plate with a little juice on it. I won't teach the curve, and I don't want the kids on my team using it."

Jack replied, "Some of the coaches allow it, but most don't. Maybe the league should be more specific, but it isn't. You coach the way you see fit."

Mike seemed pleased that his dad was going to coach the team. After talking to Lenore and his law partners, Marty accepted the coaching offer.

Marty's knowledge and love of the game overcame much of his inexperience as a coach. He remembered a lot from his own competitive years, especially his college experience, and modeled his training and field management techniques on those of his old coach but with far more patience and attention to basic skill development. Marty valued winning and was as competitive as anyone, but he felt that his main job was to help the kids develop physically and mentally and master the basics of the game. When he told all his pitchers "no curves!" there was some griping. After Marty started working hard with his hurlers on their fundamentals, the objections faded away.

Preseason practice went well. The team's strengths were pitching and speed; it's only major weakness was a lack of power hitting. Overall, it was a good team, and the kids seemed to be coming together as a unit. The experience gave Mike and Marty a lot more to talk about at home. On the field, both were careful not to make anything special of their father/son relationship. But at the dinner table, most of the conversation revolved around baseball. Lenore and Mike's older sister, Ellen, just smiled and put up with it, remembering their stint as player and coach a few years earlier.

The first tournament of the season for the traveling team—three games over a single weekend—was in a town about thirty miles away. Marty was amazed and thrilled that over a hundred people, not all of them relatives of the players, had made the trip to cheer on the team. The Sterns' first game as coach and player was a win. Entering the game as a pinch hitter, Mike walked and scored a run. Marty overcame his rookie jitters to coach what he felt was a game largely free of tactical errors. Mike started the second game and lasted four innings before giving up three runs on five solid hits in the fifth. The team ultimately lost.

In the final game, the starting pitcher for Marty's team pitched a very strong game. With the score 2–1 in the last half-inning, the opposing team loaded the bases on two singles and a walk. The first pitch to the next batter was a good curve ball for a strike. Marty immediately called time, walked to the mound, and asked the catcher, who had also walked to the mound, "Did you call for that curve?" The pitcher told Marty that he had thrown it on his own. Marty put his hand out for the ball and told his pitcher, "Nice job, but you know our rules. Go sit down. I'll talk to you later." The reliever walked the next two batters, and the team lost.

On the bus ride home, Marty spent most of the time with the pitcher he had pulled. He explained again his opposition to kids throwing curves at too young an age and expressed confidence in the pitcher for the next tournament. The youngster was visibly upset and angry but said nothing. Mike was more outspoken when he and his dad were alone. "Dad, how can we win if the other team is using the curve and we can't? I don't think it's fair!"

"Mike, not everything is fair. I told you guys up front that the curve was out. I don't want my pitchers to screw up their arms by rushing into a pitch that could hurt them before they have mastered their basic motion and learned to throw the fastball for strikes."

Mike grumbled some more, and Marty finally had to shut the subject off.

That night, Marty received over a dozen phone calls from irate parents and others who accused Marty of blowing the game by removing the starting pitcher. The next day before practice, Jack Wilson called Marty aside and told him, "You know, Marty, this isn't Little League any more. These young people are expected to compete at a higher level and to win a good number of games. There's nothing in the rules of this league against throwing curve balls. Other teams allow curves, and we need to be competitive with them. Of course, I'm not trying to tell you how to coach, but...."

Marty replied, "Well, Jack, there may be no rule against it, but I told you—and I told the team—I wouldn't allow curves in practices or in games."

The chairman angrily left the field.

Two more weekend tournaments came and went, and the team was improving. Its record stood at 5—4, and the kids seemed to be having a good time. Then Mike threw several curves in a practice game. Marty, after warning him, told him he would miss his next start. Needless to say, things were a bit crisp at home: Mike and Marty got into an angry confrontation in front of the rest of the family, which only ended when Mike stormed out of the house. Of course, word immediately spread that Marty had suspended his own son, one of the team's best pitchers. The phone calls and complaints started again in earnest.

One afternoon, Mike sat down with his mother. "It's not the big deal Dad is making it out to be, mom. Everyone my age fools around with curves and sliders and even screwballs. It would be better if Dad would teach us the right way, and maybe we would win a few more games, too."

Lenore replied, "Mike, your father is worried about you hurting your arm, and he has your best interests at heart."

"Mom, if we threw nine innings of nothing but curves and other junk, okay, maybe we'd get hurt; but practicing it once in a while and using it a few times in a game isn't going to do anything bad. Just talk to him, okay?"

That evening, Marty got home late from a court case and sighed as he plunked down in his chair. "I'm not sure which is worse, opposing counsel hammering at my client all day or a bunch of people who think they know more than the coach hammering at me on the phone. I hope that dies down again. Well, a quick bite, and I'm off to practice."

While Marty and Mike were at practice, Lenore realized that Marty hadn't been home for an uninterrupted evening in weeks and was tied up every weekend with games and tournaments. She also realized that the only real conversation she had had with Mike since the season started was that afternoon. Sure it was about baseball, but he really had opened up to his mother. She resolved to talk to Marty about the way Mike felt.

The following Friday evening, the game was rained out. Mike took the opportunity to go over to a friend's house, Ellen went out on a date, and Lenore and Marty had an evening to themselves at home.

Perhaps the last thing Marty had on his mind for the evening was a discussion of the appropriate use of the curve by thirteen-year-olds, but that's just what happened. Lenore told Marty about her conversation with Mike. "He feels really bad, dear. He just doesn't think it will hurt to throw a few curves. He thinks you are too rigid on the subject."

"You bet I'm rigid," Marty replied. "I've seen kids who blew out their arms at sixteen because they threw the curve improperly or too much. They've messed up their chances to go on in baseball or a lot of other sports. Here, let me show you some of the things that the sports medicine people say."

"I don't want to read a bunch of stuff, Marty. But if it's so bad, why does the league allow it?"

"You and Mike really have been having at it, haven't you?" said Marty, who was now just a bit hot under the collar. "I can't control the league.

They obviously have ducked the issue. I can't control our association, either. Jack Wilson has been giving me a real hard time. All I can do is to coach the way I believe is best for the team and the individuals—although I'm beginning to wonder if it's worth it. Mike is mad at me and taking his gripes to you. Other parents call all the time to complain. I can't walk down the street without someone giving me crap. Now you and I are arguing over the damn curve, and that's the last thing I want.

"I really understand now why it's so tough to get people to volunteer to coach kids' teams. Even coaching thirteen-year-olds, I have to put up with a whole lot I didn't expect.

"Let's make a deal. I'm not a quitter, and I'm not going to walk out on the kids. But let's not let Mike use you to make his points with me. And I promise that, after this season, no more coaching. You did it for a year, I'll do it for a year, then we've paid our dues!"

Lenore agreed that making this a short-term obligation would be the best thing for them as a couple and family. Later, she read some of the sports medicine articles that Marty had recommended. Although she thought that Marty was being perhaps a bit conservative in his approach to the issue, she understood that his motives were good: to protect the welfare of the kids, including their son.

Things came to a head sooner than any of the Stern family expected. Marty was requested to attend the next community athletic association board meeting, at which the board members discussed requiring Marty to allow his pitchers to throw curves. Marty asked each of the seven board members, "What's the goal of this program? If it is to develop the youth of the community as our mission statement says, then fine. We work on the fundamentals of pitching, and we don't let thirteen-year-olds throw curves. If it's to win as many games as possible, which sure seems to be the way you people are talking, then let the pitchers throw curves. But first, find a new coach and don't come running back to me when a kid blows his arm out at seventeen."

A solid majority of the board voted to require the coach of the traveling team to teach and permit the use of the curve ball, since it wasn't specifically prohibited in the rules of the league.

Marty resigned the next day. His assistant took over and immediately began to implement the new policy. Marty told his son to either find another position on the team or quit because, speaking as a father and not as a coach, Marty would not let Mike throw curves. Mike argued with Marty. The situation between them became even more strained. The boy tried a couple of more times to influence his father through his mother, but she told him that it was a joint decision that he not use the curve.

Mike withdrew from both his parents for quite some time. He did decide to stay with his buddies on the team, and his strong arm allowed him make a quick transition to playing third base. The new coach also used him to good effect as a fastball-throwing relief pitcher when he needed one or two outs. The team went on to finish second in the league. Once in a while Mike fantasized about winning the championship game by striking out the other team's leading slugger with a roundhouse curve—but not often. He and his buddies moved on to other sports when the baseball season ended.

Mike gradually fell back into his typical thirteen-year-old ways, griping to his friends about how out of it his parents were and what a weirdo his sister had become. To throw a curve or not to throw a curve ceased to be a contentious issue, and things slowly got back to normal—normal that is for a family with two active parents and two active teens. The whole episode had at least one positive effect. It convinced Marty and Lenore to talk more to each other so one of them could not be used as an advocate against the other by the children.

Lenore and Marty continued to support both their children and were frequently seen in the stands cheering for the home team. Neither of them ever coached youth sports again.

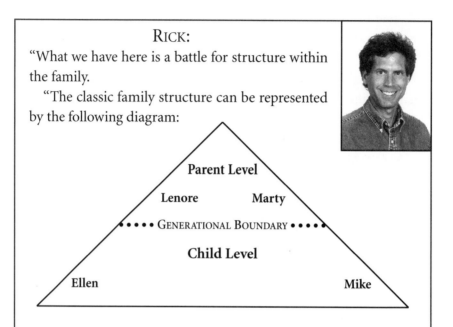

RICK:
"What we have here is a battle for structure within the family.

"The classic family structure can be represented by the following diagram:

"This shows the generational boundary functioning properly. The parents—Lenore and Marty—are on their side of the line, and the children—Ellen and Mike—are on the other side.

"Now see what happens when Mike tries to align himself with Lenore against Marty:

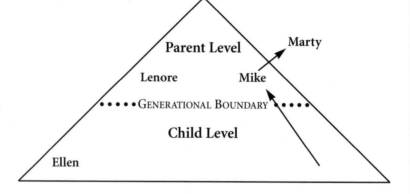

"Mike moves across the generational boundary, weakening it. Ellen is alone and feeling isolated in the Child Level. Not only does Marty feel that his space has been invaded by his son, but he feels that he is being moved out of the hierarchy completely.

"Sometimes in a situation like this, the displaced adult will try to form an alliance with another child as a way of getting back into the structure. Unfortunately, this doesn't address the basic problem: A child is still on the Parent Level and he doesn't belong there.

"Marty handles this situation adroitly. He sees the split developing between him and his wife, and he moves to prevent it. Because they communicate well, the parents are able to move Mike out of the Parent Level, despite his resistance, and back to the Child Level where he belongs, thus restoring a healthy balance within the family.

"There's another issue here complicating these family relationships, and that's the issue of sports itself. Right now, all the family seems to talk about is sports. I would worry that Mike might someday wonder if his family knows who he is outside of sports. One of the positive outcomes in this case is that the family will almost certainly become less obsessed with baseball and return to a broader range of conversational topics."

JOHN:

"Coaching your own child impacts the entire family. It is difficult to be both the even-handed coach who treats all his players alike and the loving father trying to bond with his own child, who just happens to be one of his players.

"When Mike's father, Marty, bans the pitchers on the traveling team from throwing curve balls, the players revolt.

Mike, being a typical teenage kid, is strongly swayed by the attitudes of his peers. 'How come your old man won't let us throw the curve?' they ask him. 'We can't win unless we can throw curves like the other teams. You gotta get to him.'

"Mike wants to win as much as anyone on the team—and he wants his friends to like him—so he goes to his mother to try to get her to take his side against Marty. Mike had begun to think of his dad as his buddy. Now that his dad isn't acting like a buddy anymore, Mike is taking his case to someone he hopes will offer a more sympathetic ear.

"Lenore loves her son and cares about him and is willing to hear him out, even though she doesn't know as much about baseball as her husband and doesn't really understand what the big deal is about kids throwing curveballs.

"The relationship between coach and player has changed the relationship between father and son, and, because of that, the son has been able to split his parents. This is not at all uncommon in families. Fortunately, in this case, the communication between father and mother and the boundaries between parent and child were strong enough to avert a major family crisis.

"Coaching can be stressful. And coaching your own kid can be particularly stressful. I guess the best advice I can give a parent coaching his or her child is to try to maintain healthy boundaries in the family. Even if you want to bond more with your child through sport, remember, you aren't your child's buddy—you are his or her parent."

Warren—Moving the Line

Throughout his life, Warren MacDermott has loved to play tennis. He started playing in junior high school and was a varsity player in both singles and doubles in high school and college. As good as he was, he always understood his limitations. He knew that he was never going to be a professional player or win a Davis Cup match. However, he didn't want to give up competitive tennis after he graduated from college with a degree in physical education, and he didn't want to become just another gym teacher in a public school somewhere. He diligently searched before he found what for him seemed the perfect job.

The Centertown Spa and Academy was a new commercial fitness club in a major city in the southwestern part of the country. In addition to offering the usual facilities, Centertown was about to open a tennis training center for young people and begin sponsoring teams in several age groups in the area club league. Warren was hired as an assistant professional by Donny Thompson, the head pro at the training center. One of his duties was to give private lessons to adult members of the spa, but his main focus was on building a program for girls divided into three levels: ages eight to eleven, twelve to fourteen, and fifteen to sixteen.

Warren and his girlfriend, Martha, with whom he had been living for a year, moved to an apartment with a spectacular view of the nearby mountains. Martha found a job as a paralegal, and both jumped head-first into their first post-college jobs with enthusiasm. Warren's salary wasn't spectacular, but he earned regular and significant tips from his private students. That, combined with Martha's much better salary, made them feel like royalty.

In coaching, Warren seemed to find his true calling. He instinctively reached back for techniques used by his former coaches, discarding what didn't work and developing an approach that was both consistent and flexible. Donny encouraged Warren to develop his own style of coaching and was pleased at the rapid progress of his young assistant.

Warren enjoyed introducing the eight-year-olds to competitive tennis and the concept of team play, and he enjoyed seeing his older girls take their skills to a higher level. In his first season, Warren's teams competed well against clubs and programs that had been established for a much longer time. His twelve- to fourteen-year-old girls even won their age bracket, and the younger and older teams both finished with winning records. Donny congratulated Warren publicly and rewarded him with an excellent performance review and a significant raise. Warren joked to Martha, "One more season like that, and I may be earning just as much as you are."

One reason for the success of the twelve-to-fourteen team was the play of thirteen-year-old Jenny Hilton. Her father had been a nationally ranked player, and her mother had just played in the doubles finals of their country club's "B" championship. The Hiltons enrolled Jenny in Centertown's tennis academy instead of a more established program because they were impressed with the facilities, with Donny's leadership, and with Warren, who would have the most direct influence on their daughter's development.

Jenny had made great strides as a player and was the leader of the team. As the number-one singles player on the team, she was unbeaten throughout the season, and, with her partner, lost only twice as the first doubles team. Warren found her to be bright, focused, and highly coachable. He talked about her to Donny. "Donny, you've been around this business a lot longer than I have. Maybe I'm just overplaying the thing, but I think Jenny has a chance to do great things in tennis. Maybe crack the pros. At the very least, if she continues progressing, she could play for a major university program. What do you think we should do next?"

Donny agreed with his young assistant. "You're not exaggerating her abilities or her potential, Warren. I think we have a player who can put this program on the national map. Let's meet with her folks first and see what level of commitment they are willing to make. Then you can talk to Jenny about her future."

The Hiltons listened to Donny and Warren with growing pride and excitement. Eric, Jenny's father, expressed his unqualified happiness to have another member of the family looking to climb the ladder of competitive tennis. Jenny's mother, Sue, raised the only caution: "She just turned fourteen, and she is at 'that' age—questioning everything we say or do and going off on her own more and more. I remember when I did that. It's not all bad, but she is very open to suggestions from people outside the family at this point. Gentlemen, I think she is in good hands with you two, but you will have to be firm with her."

Donny and Warren assured Mrs. Hilton that they would be firm with Jenny. When Warren met with Jenny over a soft drink at the academy, he outlined a rigorous program of conditioning, specialized lessons, and practice, practice, practice. "You won't have much time for other activities, Jenny. Between your schoolwork and tennis, it's going to be a demanding regime. Both Donny and I think, and your mom and dad agree, that you have talent and should be given every opportunity to see how far you can go in this sport."

Jenny happily agreed to the program and was especially pleased that she would get to spend a lot more time with Warren. She felt he really understood her.

The next few months were a blur to Warren. He rose at 4:30 a.m. and raced to the academy by 5:30 for conditioning exercises with Jenny and two other players, both boys, whom Donny had placed on the same fast track. After the conditioning exercises, he had time for some drills with Jenny before she left for school and his "real" day of group and private lessons for adults began. His work with Jenny started again at 3:00 in the afternoon and lasted until 6:30 or 7:00 in the evening. Jenny seemed to thrive on the schedule, and on the personal attention her coach was giving her. Warren saw real improvement in almost all phases of her game. The only problem was that at times, her head seemed to be anywhere but on the task at hand. When he brought the problem to Jenny's attention, she threw down her racquet and stormed off the court in tears.

That evening, Warren told Martha what had happened. "It's a phase," Martha said. "We all have been through it. She is growing up and trying out a little independence. And from what you've told me about her parents, especially her dad, I bet that isn't sitting too well at home. The Hiltons may feel a little shut out right now since they are no longer directly involved in Jenny's coaching. Try to be a little patient with her. You've got her life moving along a very narrow path right now. Maybe she is rebelling a little at that, too."

Warren thought Martha's advice was right on the mark. Heck, Martha and he were still only in their mid-twenties, and when Warren thought back to some of the things he had done as a teen to prove his independence, he cringed. He would cut Jenny some slack and try to be more understanding.

The next morning, Jenny showed up on time at 5:30 a.m. and went through morning conditioning and drills without comment. That afternoon, Warren intercepted her as she was starting out onto the practice court. "Jenny, let's have a talk before practice. I didn't like what happened yesterday. I suspect you didn't, either."

As they sat on a bench, Jenny first apologized for her outburst and then opened up to Warren that she was having real problems with her parents, mostly her father. "He just wants to control every minute of my life when I'm not here, and then he needs to hear about everything I do at the academy, especially any mistakes I make. I don't like it. Mom's no help. All I want is a little space. I am almost fifteen, you know."

"Yeah, in ten months," Warren thought, though he really sympathized with Jenny. Her problems weren't much different from those he had experienced at the same age, and he told her so. "Jenny, I don't in any way want to undermine your parent's relationship with you, but if you want to talk to someone, I'm here for you." Jenny thanked him, and they went off to practice.

It was not long after Warren's well-intentioned offer to Jenny that he began to feel uncomfortable. He was afraid that he might have crossed a line. Jenny was calling him almost every evening, pouring her heart out to him about her problems with her folks. Even Martha commented, "This is a little more than a phase. She has latched on to you. This could be trouble. Plus, you and I don't have a lot of hours together. I don't think we need to be constantly interrupted by your protégé's problems."

The next few weeks were difficult for Warren. Not only did Jenny attach herself to him at every opportunity, but he could swear she was flirting. Their discussions had progressed into areas that were uncomfortably personal. One afternoon when practice was over, Jenny disclosed some intimate details of a sexual encounter she had recently. Then she asked Warren about his sex life. Was he really committed to Martha?

Warren knew he was on the wrong track with Jenny. Somewhat reluctant and embarrassed, he sought the counsel of Donny Thompson. "Boss, I don't know what I've done, but this situation is getting out of hand. I don't know how to bring things around without losing the ability to be a coach and friend to Jenny. She needs guidance, but I'm not her father, and I'm certainly not her boyfriend. What is going on now is making me very uncomfortable, and I know I'm not helping Jenny. I need your help."

Donny let out a sigh and said, "Warren, most coaches with twice your experience wouldn't have sensed trouble as soon as you have. Nothing that you have told me, nothing I've observed, changes my mind about your future in coaching. But you are absolutely correct. The situation with Jenny is not yet out of control, but if we don't do something, it will be. Have you ever heard about the coaching pyramid, Warren?"

"No, what is it?"

"A sports psychologist who spoke at a coaching clinic a few years ago showed this to me. At first I didn't think much about it. But, in the past year or so, I've used it as a guide in a couple of situations similar to the one you're in with Jenny. Here, let me draw it out for you."

Donny sketched the following on a piece of paper.

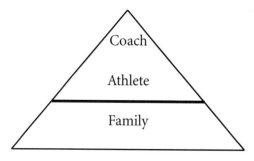

"This is the way things are now with you, Jenny, and the Hiltons," Donny explained. "It's only natural that Jenny begin to show independence at her age, but what she's done is to draw a solid line between her and her folks. Because you offered to be a friend and sounding board as well as a coach, you've helped her break down the line that should exist between the two of you. Warren, that line has to be there. You are her coach, nothing more. There's nothing wrong with showing concern for a player's feelings. Being close to the kids is why most of us are in this profession. We like kids. We want to help them excel.

"What you have to do, Warren, is reestablish a definite line between coach and player. To do this, you need to remove the line that's been drawn between athlete and family and redraw it between coach and athlete. My suggestion is to involve the parents more in Jenny's training. When we started coaching Jenny, both Eric and Sue got the idea that they should stay away from the training center when Jenny was going through her workouts and instruction. And we did nothing to discourage that idea. After all, it's easier to get started with a student if you don't have the parents around. But now you are in an uncomfortable position, and I wouldn't be surprised if the Hiltons already suspect that you are the one Jenny is confiding in, since she isn't confiding in them anymore.

"Why don't you have Jenny take a note home to her parents? In the note, mention how much progress Jenny has made as a player and how you have appreciated Eric and Sue's cooperation during the first stage of training. But now you and Jenny would like her folks to observe practice and see for themselves what wonderful tennis talent their daughter has. Make sure Jenny knows what is in the note. Then follow up with a phone call if you don't hear back soon—though, I suspect that Eric, at least, will be at the next session.

"You need to accomplish two things. First, you need to change the parents' perspective so that they see you as a coach and not a confessor. You need to reassure them of your professionalism where their daughter is concerned. Second, you need to change Jenny's perspective so that she sees that the line she's drawn between her and her parents is being moved back into its proper position between her and her coach. She may, at first, feel betrayed and let down. She may withdraw from you when you don't make yourself available to her anytime she wants to talk. That's fine, and that's where you can be a real pro by maintaining your cool and your professional demeanor as a coach. Hopefully, a few weeks of her folks participating in practices will help the family start talking again—but, the truth is, that's not your problem.

"If this works, the coaching pyramid should look like this."

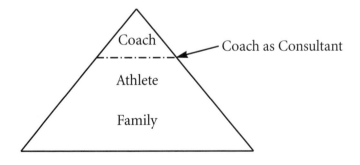

"You can see," Donny continued, "that the boundary between coach and player doesn't have to be a solid line, but it does have to be some kind of line, and it has to be respected and maintained. A smart coach never forgets that he's a consultant, not a family member. You wisely sensed something was wrong almost as soon as the boundary between you and Jenny began to break down.

"I put a dotted line between Jenny and her folks. I hope there will be some breaks in the big thick wall Jenny has built between herself and her folks, but that's something we can't control and, to a degree, shouldn't try to. After all, some line between the generations is beneficial in the sense that it signifies privacy and mutual respect."

Warren sat and stared at both pyramids. Then he shook his head and turned to his boss and mentor. "Thanks, Donny. I knew something wasn't right, but I didn't have the experience to know how to handle it. You've helped me to get my head straight on what to do."

As Warren was leaving, he turned and said to Donny, "I bet you it takes me a lot longer to put those pyramid things into practice with the Hilton clan than it did for you to tell me about them!"

Warren's note to the Hiltons brought the expected results. Both Eric and Sue became regular visitors to the training center. Only once did Warren have to caution Eric not to be so supportive that he interfered with Jenny's concentration. During the next several weeks, it appeared to Warren that Jenny was getting the message about respecting the boundary between coach and player. One day she told him, "I'm sorry I was dumping everything on you. I really think you are a great coach."

Warren said, "Everyone needs someone to talk to sometime. But my main job is to help you become the very best tennis player possible. I know your parents would prefer if you went to them to talk about the things that are important in your life."

When Jenny returned to the center after a holiday weekend, she was focused and enthusiastic. She listened to Warren as he coached her, but

Warren couldn't tell whether there was any lingering problems between them or between her and her parents.

Part of the answer came in a most unexpected manner. He came home one evening to a smiling Martha and a beautiful bouquet. "Well, honey," he said, "I'd like to take the credit, but it looks like you have attracted the eye of another man."

"Read the card, Warren," Martha replied.

> *Dear Martha,*
>   *Thank you for helping Warren be such a neat and together person. He's a great coach to me and a great soulmate to you.*
>   *And he helped teach me the difference.*
>   *Love to you both,*
>   *Jenny*

JOHN:

"This is the story of a young coach who does it right. From my perspective, the first thing that Warren had going for him was a mentor. Warren didn't coach alone. He had another person he could go to so that he didn't have to figure things all out by himself.

"Many coaches, regardless of their experience, think they have all the answers. Believe me, it's so much better when you have a mentor like Donny to help.

"I like the fact that Warren, unlike our volleyball coach Alex, didn't have to be hit over the head with the facts. He realized very quickly that by telling Jenny he 'was there for her' he had potentially blurred the line between coach and player. Jenny used this opening to try to make Warren into something he didn't want to be, and Warren knew he needed help.

"Warren went to both his mentor, Donny, and his significant other, Martha, to provide him with advice and guidance. He could go to them because his relationship with each was open, honest, and secure.

"Donny helped Warren through the situation as a mentor, not as a boss. He suggested solutions rather than telling Warren what to do.

"It's not just young coaches or assistants that need sounding boards. Sometimes it's the older or head coach who can benefit from timely advice. I recently had a run-in with an umpire in the first game of a series. I was really upset. The next day, still angry, I decided to go over before the start of the game and let the umpire know how I felt. One of my assistants pulled me aside and said, 'John, think this through. Is it worth it to tell the guy off? First, wouldn't it do more harm than good to have the guy mad at us, and, second, wouldn't it throw the concentration of our team off?' He was being a consultant to me. He didn't tell me what to do; he gave me some clues. And he was right.

"In the same way that Donny helped Warren figure things out for himself, Warren now is helping Jenny figure things out for herself. He is giving her clues that point her in the right direction, but he isn't dragging her to the answers. He is teaching by giving his pupil a chance to learn. He's suggesting, not telling.

"The coach can provide pieces of the puzzle, but the player has to put the pieces together. Jenny is responsible for changing her own behavior and for rebuilding her relationship with her parents.

"It's very easy for a coach to become emotionally attached to his players and to attempt to take on problems that are better left to the parents or to trained experts like Rick. As coaches, we do have to be sensitive to the problems of our players because many times, when performance goes down, it's a problem from the neck up. But we have to be sure that the help we offer is appropriate and focused solely on getting the player's performance back on track."

RICK:

"John is right when he says coaches shouldn't take on the role of parent or professional therapist. However, coaches can function effectively as social therapists. A social therapist is a nonprofessional who, because of his or her social relationship with you, plays an important and influential role in your life. A social therapist can be a teacher, a coach, a relative, or a friend. He or she is usually older or more experienced than you are, rather than a peer.

"We all have our social therapists. Most of us could probably name three or four people who act as social therapists in our lives. Whenever we're in a difficult spot, we tend to go to these people. We trust them to be up front and honest with us. They may not tell us what we want to hear, but, rather, what we ought to hear. They can see through our cover and get to the heart of the situation directly.

"You are usually aware when you are acting as a mentor to someone, but you may have no idea when you are acting as a social therapist. Others, particularly younger people, may be looking up to and modeling their behavior after you without your knowledge. That's why coaching is such a critical activity. You never know for sure which kids you are affecting, or how. I've known many instances where an ex-player has asked a former coach to be a member of his or her wedding party. That's a big deal. The coach was more to that person than just someone who taught them how to play a game.

"A coach may consciously choose to act as a mentor to a player, but a coach cannot choose to act as a player's social therapist. The player chooses the coach as a social therapist. The coach may be chosen whether he or she likes it or not. You may sense that a relationship is developing between you and a player, but you can never be sure that the player thinks of you as a social therapist until he or she asks you for guidance and help.

"However tempting it may be to act as a professional therapist, a coach should rarely get involved in issues that require the expertise of a trained psychologist. To do so is, once again, to cross the line. Probably the best thing you can do for any current or former player who needs help dealing with chemical dependency, criminal behavior, depression, family problems, or similar issues is to recommend professional assistance. Making a referral is not abandoning the athlete. It's natural to want to help your kids bear their burdens, but, if you take too much on your shoulders, you can be dragged under. You have to know your limitations. Pay attention to your own comfort level.

"In the preceding case study, Warren knew his limitations in acting as a social therapist to Jenny. And he was lucky enough to have a social therapist of his own he could go to for good advice. Donny was also an excellent consultant to Warren; sometimes we need someone we trust to tell us, "Don't even think of going down that path." And because Donny was consciously guiding Warren from the perspective of an older and more experienced coach, he was also acting as a mentor to Warren.

"Unfortunately, not everyone has a "Donny" they can turn to in times of trouble. We do a poor job of teaching our young coaches about the gray areas and boundaries of coaching as they go through school and certification programs. We lose coaches all the time because they slip too far into a sticky situation and can't get out."

Susan Lands a Superstar

Susan Pytleski has been the head coach of a Division I university softball program for five years. The program is successful but, for a variety of reasons, is not considered one of the nation's elite. Susan mostly recruits locally, within a corridor between New York City and Washington, D.C. A few players are from other areas, but they're generally walk-ons who have come to the university for reasons other than to play softball. Susan's program usually does not attract the premiere high school athletes, even from this limited recruiting area.

Susan herself had been a walk-on player at a similar program in the Missouri Valley and had begun coaching as an assistant at her alma mater. When her present school was looking for a new softball coach, they approached Sam Fortier, her college coach and mentor. The recruiter, an assistant athletic director, told Sam on the side that they really were under some pressure to hire a female as the new head coach. Sam replied, "You can talk to her. She's a good coach with very good people skills, and I think, for the most part, she's ready for you. I'd like to see her get more seasoning as an assistant, but it's a good opportunity for her. Just one bit of advice: I wouldn't mention anything about the pressure to hire a female coach. Susan would tell you where to get off if she thought she was being considered primarily because she's a woman."

Susan agreed to a contract with her new school after talking with the assistant A.D. and visiting the campus. She moved from her native Kansas to the East Coast.

Her first several years were spent rebuilding a program that had suffered from neglect. She learned the subtle and not-so-subtle ways to get funds from the administration for upkeep and repairs on her practice and game fields. She successfully lobbied for access to the sacrosanct indoor football training facility. The words "Title IX" carried a lot of impact, though Susan used this hammer sparingly. One day in her second year,

Tom Gustavson, the head baseball coach, dropped in to her office. "I wanted to thank you, Susan. Nice work."

"What nice work, Tom?"

"Well, when you used the Title IX can opener and got the A.D. to tell our revenue-producing football coach to open up his temple to your team, I figured 'what the hell, let's see if this equality stuff cuts both ways.' And you know what? It does! At least we now can get on the schedule to work out indoors, too. So thank you, Ms. Pytleski, thank you."

"That's great, Tom," Susan replied. "We 'nonrevenue' folks have to stick together."

Susan was popular among most of the other coaches at the university. Even the football coach finally admitted that she was a pro and had done a good job advocating for her team. Her record, which was 7–33 her first season, rose to 16–16 during her second year, and she was named "coach of the year" by her league.

Even recruiting, which Susan thought to be her weakest area as a coach, was picking up. Recruiting within a fairly narrow geographic area, she brought in a couple of very good pitchers, one of whom she stole from under the nose of the enormous state university. That recruit, Kaley Jones, told the state university coach that she had just felt more comfortable with Susan, who seemed to think of her more as a person than a cog in a large machine.

The third season brought Susan's best record, 22–13, and a trip to the league tournament, where her team lost in the semifinals. Kaley Jones and the other freshman pitcher, Amy Perkins, were named to the all-conference first and second teams, respectively.

As soon as the season ended, Susan began to think about the makeup of the team for the next season and beyond. Pitching looked pretty stable. There was power throughout the line-up, and the infield was tight defensively. Catcher—that was the big void. Her three-year starter was graduating, and her backup really wasn't at a skill level to help move the team up in the rankings. Susan thought she had the answer but wasn't certain: Angela Baffa.

Susan grinned wryly and turned to Ben Warren, her assistant coach. "Well, Ben, do you think our Ms. All-Everything is going to reward me for being her big sister and mother confessor?"

Ben didn't smile back. "Susan, she's verbally committed to us, but until she walks on to campus, registers, and actually shows up at fall practice, I wouldn't count on her. I'm going to keep on hammering at a couple of uncommitted kids and the one junior college catcher we still have a shot at."

The object of their conversation and concern, Angela Baffa, was a seventeen-year-old catcher for the Class A school champions of a neighboring state. Angela had it all: size; quickness; power; a strong, accurate arm; and leadership skills. She also had a 3.1 G.P.A. and decent test scores.

These qualities made her not only the recruit of choice for Susan but for many other schools, including the California institution whose softball program was coached by the legendary Jack Gowler. Gowler's teams seemed always to be in the final hunt for the NCAA championship and had won it two out of the past four seasons.

Angela was the type of national-level recruit that Susan and the university had historically had trouble signing. The more glamourous national programs had inevitably lured them away, even when the athletes had made verbal commitments. But Susan had thought from her first meeting that she had a chance to land Angela.

The Baffa girl's accomplishments on the field and in the classroom belied a very sad and stressful home life. Her mother died giving birth to Angela's brother, and her father deserted the family when his wife died. Angela and her brother, Joe, were raised by their maternal grandparents, who didn't know how to handle a seventeen-year-old girl trying to cope with national publicity and over forty college recruiters, much less a troubled fourteen-year-old boy who had grown up believing that he was responsible for his mother's death. Where Angela used athletics as an outlet, Joe had turned to alcohol and drugs.

Susan knew all this before she approached Angela and her grandparents. Amy Perkins, one of the team's pitchers, had gone to another high school in Angela's home town and had played with her in a summer development program. They had become friends, and Angela had told Amy some of her problems during a road trip where they were roommates. "She's for real as a player," Amy told Susan, "and she is really a good person. She just has no one to talk to. Her grandparents don't have a clue, her high school coach is as old as her grandparents, and her brother is constantly in treatment or hanging out with the other druggies. We still send each other e-mail once in a while."

One thing became very clear as Susan planned her "land Baffa" strategy: This youngster was going to require careful handling, constant attention, and considerable time and effort if the university was going to have a chance to sign her.

"Well, kiddo," Susan thought to herself, "we will really be reaching for the moon with this one, but, what the hell, we need a catcher and I'm pretty good at getting close to potential recruits. Most of my colleagues are still men and I think that gives me an edge in this situation. My style may yet win out over the hard sell."

Susan's first thought was that Angela had probably seen enough glossy recruiting packages. As an alternative, she sent a personal note to Angela via the Internet to introduce herself. She didn't try to push Angel; she simply asked if she could meet her to discuss if there might be a fit between Angela's needs and the university's programs.

Angela was flattered and intrigued. She had been receiving recruiting materials since the tenth grade and had already made all but one of her allowed campus visits. She had always seen herself as the star of a national championship team. That meant going to one of the top programs. "However," she thought, "this coach sounds a little different. She hardly mentioned her program and didn't try to sell me on the university." She e-mailed back, agreeing to a meeting.

Susan telephoned Angela's home and made an appointment with both Angela and her grandparents. As soon as Susan was in the home, Angela said, "Thanks for the e-mail. It was nice. I felt like I was meeting a friend rather than another recruiter when you knocked on the door today."

After the meeting with Angela's grandparents, she and Susan went to a local coffee shop to continue their discussion. During the next several hours, Angela opened up to Susan about her home life, her frustrations, and her goals. "My grandparents are really great, don't get me wrong. They have tried to do what's best for my brother and me, but they just don't understand what it's like. When my mother was growing up, girls just didn't have the opportunities to play sports they have today.

"I guess you know about my brother. Everyone tells me to just forget about him and get on with my life. But how can I just walk away from him? He's really screwed up, and I think I'm the only lifeline he has."

Susan talked about her high school and college years and some of her successes and failures on the field and in life. She said very little about the needs of her softball program but did indicate that she would welcome a return visit by Angela to the university. They both were surprised when they realized four hours had passed.

Angela finally said, "Susan, it's been great talking to you. I have one recruiting visit left. I'd love to come to your university and visit you."

"That's great," Susan replied. "We'll make sure you get a good sense of the place, check out the environment, see if you feel comfortable. If you want to take a look at anything on campus, just ask. Amy and Kaley will be your guides. And, of course, I'll talk to you before you leave."

Angela Baffa's visit could not have gone better. The team was in the middle of the fall practice schedule, but there was plenty else going on, too, and Amy and Kaley made sure Angela saw and did as much as possible. The morning Angela was to leave, Amy called Susan. "We showed her a good time, and I think we were straight with her, Coach. She likes the campus but isn't sure our program is big time enough for her. I think she would be signed by one of the California schools by now if she hadn't met you. You two really must have gotten along great. I hope you land her."

Susan took Angela to a quiet off-campus restaurant for lunch and a final talk. Once again, hours passed quickly, and Angela felt more and more that she could have a special relationship with this coach. Susan listened, wasn't quick to judge, and asked insightful questions. She seemed to Angela to be part mother, part big sister, and part coach. When it came time for her to leave, Angela said to Susan, "Part of me wants to go out West where they battle for the championship every year. Part of me wants to come here and help you build a program. I just don't know. I don't think I'm going to make a decision right now. I'll wait until the spring. You will keep in touch, won't you? And I don't mean as a recruiter!"

Susan replied, "Of course, I'll keep in touch. The NCAA only allows us to telephone you once a week, but I will sure do that."

Later that week, Susan thought about the e-mail contact again and how effective it had been. She went down the hall and spoke with Ken Still, the compliance officer for the woman's athletic programs. "Ken, I'm not as up as I should be on communication by computer. One of our possible recruits is a national-level player from our region. Just the type we usually lose to the big universities. I know I can only telephone her once a week, but what about e-mail?"

Ken bestowed on Susan one of his rare smiles. "Susan, the whole Internet thing, including e-mail, is a loophole in the current recruiting rules. You can send her e-mail every day if you want. It's weird, but the NCAA hasn't put computer communication in the same class as telephone calls, faxes, and personal visits. Treat your e-mail just like U.S. mail as far as the rules are concerned, but with one big difference. You know you can't include things like game programs in a regular letter to a prospect, but there is nothing in the rules against you directing a recruit's attention to our wonderful university web site and to the very informative pages maintained by this athletic department."

Susan used both her weekly phone calls and more frequent e-mails to continue her relationship with Angela—an emotionally draining relationship for the young coach as Angela came more and more to depend on Susan for advice on everything from her relationship with her grandparents to her brother's latest problem. Susan began to wonder whether the need for a top-level player like Angela was worth the tremendous effort it seemed to require. As the spring signing period loomed, Angela asked Susan for a short period of no contact. She told the coach she had asked Jack Gowler, her other finalist, the same. "I need the time just to think. I still am torn between the two programs. I really want Gowler to lay off the hard sell. I think it's only fair if we don't talk, either, until I make up my mind."

Susan agreed. "Angela, we would like you to come here, but I also want what you think will be best for you. You know I will respect your decision."

The day before the signing period ended, Susan was in her office trying once more to put the puzzle together of what her team would look like in the coming year. The phone rang. It was Angela. "Well, Susan, Jack Gowler just called to put the heat on me one more time to come West to play for him. He is a good coach with great facilities and a super program. But he didn't respect my request to back off so I could think a little. I think I can get more by playing for you, and not just in softball. If you want a catcher, you've got her."

Susan was actually trembling as she thanked Angela for her decision. She reviewed with her what paperwork needed to be done and, when she put down the phone, Susan screamed "Yahoo!" at the top of her lungs. A big piece of the puzzle had been solved.

For the next several months, Angela called Susan with increasing frequency. The two had built a bond and genuinely liked each other. Angela filled Susan in on her last weeks of high school, graduation, and her summer plans, including her softball schedule. Angela commented that she had chosen to come to the university mainly because of the special relationship she had with Susan.

That comment bothered Susan a bit at the time. She hoped there would be lots of other reasons for Angela to enjoy her years at the university and in the softball program.

Angela's first few weeks on campus as one of 3,500 freshmen was a shock. There was no one to hold her hand and help acclimate her to dorm and classroom life. She and Susan met briefly and, while Susan was as warm and friendly as ever, something had changed.

Just what had changed and by how much became evident when fall practice started. Angela was one of about thirty women who were trying to make the first cut for the team. Angela wasn't worried about that, but she was concerned that Susan didn't seem to have enough time for her—not so much as an athlete as a friend.

Susan also was concerned for Angela. The young woman maintained a tough veneer, yet Susan knew she had a very fragile ego. During the second week of practice, she sought Angela out and asked her to come by her townhouse that evening for dinner. Angela was thrilled and thought, "Maybe things will be as special as they were before I got to campus."

At dinner, Angela told Susan how hard it was adjusting to college life. Susan listened and was sympathetic, remembering her own introduction to higher education not that many years before. "It's a challenge, Angie, but it also is part of becoming an independent adult. I'll help if I can. You know how to find me."

Susan did help, continuing her role as a surrogate big sister and advisor to Angela and helping her in many ways not directly connected with the team. As fall slipped into winter, Susan had more things to handle than she had time or energy for. The season-opening tournament in California was only five weeks away, recruiting activities were increasing, and several players were facing academic and other school-related problems. While all this was going on, Susan continued to spend a lot of her emotional capital on Angela and struggled, without much success, to have a life independent of her players.

One evening, Susan confided in her friend Carl, "I really like Angela, but I spend as much time with her as I do with the other seventeen members of the team combined. It's really beginning to burn me out. Some of the others on the squad are jealous and a bit resentful of the relationship Angela has with me."

Carl told her, "You have to pull back a little. Angela is a great kid, but she has so many needs, she's going to suck you dry. You've shown her something she never had with her parents or her grandparents, and she wants all she can get."

With the excitement of the season opener just ahead, Susan was able to limit her contact with Angela. The tournament was held on the California campus of the school Angela had turned down. Angela introduced Susan to Jack Gowler, the head coach, and the three had a pleasant conversation. Gowler's team was significantly ahead of Susan's in training because of better weather, better facilities, and, on the whole, better players. Gowler's teams won all three games against Susan's team by large margins.

Although Susan's team returned from the California with only a 2–8 record, the two wins came in the final three games. The rest of the season, however, was a grind for Susan. Practices, games, and, most of all, The Other Stuff: Angela on the phone, Angela in the office, Angela before a game, Angela after practice. Every time Susan tried to create a little space between herself and Angela, Angela reacted with resentment. The coach was picking on her on the field, Angela thought, and ignoring her off the field. In fact, Susan was just trying to move Angela toward taking some control over her own life.

The team finished the season 26–10. A good record, but not good enough to qualify for the NCAA tournament. Angela's play had deteriorated during the season, and Susan had benched her for two games. Everyone could see that she wasn't showing the same enthusiasm and diligence she's shown at the start of the season.

Before returning home for the summer, Angela had a long conversation with Susan. "I guess maybe I was naïve, but I thought you and I could continue our friendship, Susan. Maybe it just can't be because I'm a player and you're the coach, but I'm not happy. I really question whether coming here was for the best."

Susan thought for a long time. "Angela, I wasn't faking my interest in you. I like you. But I can't be everything you want me to be and coach seventeen other players and recruit and do the other things I have to do. You are a special person and I enjoy coaching you, but you need to make your own decisions."

The meeting ended quickly as Angela just shook her head in denial and walked out of Susan's office.

After Angela left campus, Susan didn't hear from her for over a month. She called her grandparents' home and found that Angela had gone to California to play summer ball. It therefore came as no surprise to Susan when she received a letter from Angela thanking her for all she had done and informing Susan and the university that she was requesting a release from her commitment and scholarship for the purpose of transferring to Jack Gowler's program. "They almost won it all this year, Susan, and I know I can play for Gowler. I hope you won't be too upset and that you will still think of me as a friend. I will never forget your kindness."

The news, while not a shock, hit Susan right in the gut. She walked around campus for several hours, feeling anger alternately toward Angela and herself. Finally she calmed down enough to send a memo to the athletic director with a copy of Angela's letter and a request that her request for a release be granted. "She's already left us," Susan wrote, "and I don't think anything would be gained by anyone by making her sit out a year. Let's give her a release and wish her good luck."

Susan walked the memo up to the director's office. When she got back, Amy, Kaley and two other players were waiting for her. "News sure travels fast these days. What did she do, Amy, send you an e-mail?"

"Yep, and she seemed more worried about how you would take the news personally than how her leaving would impact the team. So, what we want to know is, who have you got your sights on to replace her? We're short at the two position again."

Susan cracked her first smile of the day. "Mercenary bunch, aren't you?"

"Coach," chimed in one of the other players, "we all know that Angie left the team before the playoffs. I mean, her body was here, but her head was miles away—about three thousand miles as it turned out!"

Kaley took up the conversation. "Look, Susan, we're no longer a bunch of freshmen with potential. Jan is going to be a senior next season, and the rest of us are juniors. The heck with potential, we can make the big tournament this season with a couple of breaks and one or two more players. So all we're saying is, well, we know how close you and Angie were, and now she has screwed us. We just don't want you to stop reaching for the better players."

"Yeah," said Jan, "like you did with me."

Everyone broke up laughing. Janine Wilson had been a walk-on who hadn't been recruited by any Division I program. She had a lot of self-confidence and raw talent and by her sophomore year not only was starting but had earned a partial scholarship.

"Okay, people," said the coach, "Ben already has his eye on several players, including a good junior college catcher, who wouldn't have even considered us if we hadn't done as well as we have over the past couple of years. You guys get on with your off-season work, and let us fill in the missing pieces. Deal?"

The players left, satisfied that their coach wasn't going to fold up over the loss of Angela Baffa.

Susan and Ben put together a pretty impressive bunch of recruits for that next season, including the junior college transfer. Susan continued to be the caring "people person" she always had been. She couldn't change her basic personality.

The team finished 33–6 that year and advanced through the regional tournament to earn its first NCAA Final Eight bid. They lost the first game, but beat Jack Gowler's team in the elimination bracket. A second loss put them out of contention for the championship, but the team had come a long way.

Angela had not been the starting catcher for the California school. She had been beaten out in practice by a freshman and had played sporadically most of the year. Apparently Gowler wasn't the coach Angela was looking for, either. Susan heard that she had dropped out of school altogether and was trying to catch on with one of the major amateur teams.

Susan felt sad for Angela. Their relationship had withered completely away after the transfer. As Susan's first blue-chip recruit, though, Angela would always hold a special place in her memories.

Coach Susan Pytleski continues to reach for great players, and with increasing success. The Final Eight appearance helped, as did a commitment from the university to spend additional dollars on field improvement, weight training facilities, and a new graduate assistant coach. Susan learned several lessons from her experience with Angela, perhaps the most valuable lesson being not to invest so much emotional capital in one recruit or player. It's not only a drain on the coach's limited resources, but it fills the player with expectations that are difficult, if not impossible, to meet.

JOHN:

"I see in Susan a lot of myself as a young head coach. When I started, I had only one part-time assistant on my staff, and I had to do much of the recruiting on my own. The more time you spend recruiting a kid, the more of yourself you invest in that kid. I'd see the kid play. I'd spend time with him and his family. I couldn't help but develop an emotional relationship with a recruit: It was almost like recruiting a friend.

"It's different now that I have more resources available to me. The assistant coaches connect early on with the recruits, and I have to actively seek out the recruits—preferably no later than when they arrive on campus—to connect with them myself.

"Having a larger staff allows me to bring more perspective to the coach-player relationship. I can be more objective than either the assistant or the player, who must interact on a much more personal basis. I also have an academic advisor associated with the team that I didn't have before. And I'm also able to call on Rick to work directly with players who could benefit from his expertise as a psychologist.

"So, unlike Susan and so many other coaches today, I don't have to be the recruiter, counselor, academic advisor, administrator, psychologist, assistant, and coach all rolled into one. In many colleges, high schools, and youth organizations, the coach is it.

"Even with a large staff, though, Susan might have found it difficult to satisfy someone as needy as Angela. Sometimes, it's not the "bad" kids—the ones who steal things, deal drugs, commit violent acts—that drain you as much as it is the 'Angelas' of the world. They will always need more care and attention than you can give, no matter how hard you try.

"How can you handle a case like this? Sometimes, the best tactic is to try to head the problem off by distancing yourself from the kid early on—what I call "de-recruiting" the recruit. While it's necessary to stay relatively close to a recruit through the signing period, after the recruit has signed you should gradually back away, creating some distance between you and the player before he or she arrives on campus. Some kids resent this, but it's necessary.

"Experience has taught me that it's best to let the kids know up front, during the recruiting process, that, though they are on a team and their coaches care about them, they are ultimately responsible for themselves. They have to go to class; they have to do their homework; they have to make it to practice on time; they have to ask for help when they need it. Most of the kids seem to respect and appreciate such candor. You know what, though? No matter what you do, some recruits are going to ignore your warnings about personal responsibility and wonder why the coach who recruited them isn't available every time they feel like talking. Some of them are going to be like Angela. They will be emotionally unable to stand on their own, and they will resent any coach who tries to make them be more independent. They might even become so upset that they leave your team. You have to be able to accept the possibility. Sometimes, it's preferable to lose a player than to drive yourself crazy trying to meet that kid's demands."

RICK:

"Susan's story dramatizes the dangers of forming emotional bonds with players. One of these dangers is becoming overly involved in a kid's life. The first message the kid hears from the coach during the recruiting process is, 'I care about you,' which, unfortunately, may or may not be sincere. The second message is, 'I will take care of you and be there for you.' Then, when the kid hits campus, reality sets in. The coach can't spend all of his or her time with one new recruit. The kid is first bewildered, then resentful.

"John talked about 'de-recruiting.' De-recruiting can be a painful process for a kid. You hear coaches talk about the kids calling them at home all the time. The kids think they can do that because of the emotional bond forged during the recruiting process. Some coaches rationalize the behavior by saying 'Well, they're only freshmen. They'll get over it soon and stop calling me.' Such rationalizing indicates that the coach hasn't started de-recruiting the player yet. The coach is still accommodating the recruit.

"In my private practice, many of my clients at first feel very dependent upon me. I try to get them to the point where they don't need me anymore. When I get fired, I know I've done my job.

"Let's look at the issue from a parenting perspective. Young children are needy. As they grow older, a good parent teaches them to be more self-reliant. If, on the other hand, a parent feeds a child's neediness into adulthood, the result is a dysfunctional adult child and a dysfunctional parenting relationship. Similar sorts of dysfunction can occur in coaching.

"Some coaches will use a dysfunctional relationship for their own purposes, manipulating needy kids until they've gotten what they want from them. Then they abandon them. The goal of de-recruiting is to take needy kids and teach them to be more self-reliant. In the long run, this benefits both the kid and the program—the kid, obviously, because he or she is more independent, and the program because self-motivated athletes are more likely to play to their full potential.

"For a number of reasons, we tend to develop closer relationships with our better players. This is especially true when we're in the early stages of our coaching career. We want so badly and try so hard to recruit a player of Angela's caliber that we cannot help but form an emotional bond with the player. But if the player is as demanding as Angela, this bond presents problems. It's difficult to accommodate the emotional needs of one player like Angela, let alone six or seven other kids with whom you've formed emotional bonds. There's just not enough time to take care of the needs of all these people and still do your job. Complicating the situation is the resentment that the other players on the team may harbor for the time you spend with a few.

"A player like Angela starts out by saying to herself, 'Coach loves me and will be there to meet all my needs. I'm going to sign with her program and play for her.' Then when the kid gets to school, she realizes that she is competing with many others for the coach's attention—a situation similar to sibling rivalry. The player wonders, 'Does Coach still love me? Let's test it out.' So she makes demand after demand on the coach's time and attention. She hopes that the coach will respond to such acts of dependency and reward them with renewed attention, thereby proving that the coach still cares about her.

"If that tactic fails, the player may ultimately declare, 'Coach doesn't love me anymore,' and decide to withdraw from the program, possibly in the hopes of finding someone who can meet her demands.

"To stay in the game, we need to be able to find a middle ground between fostering dependency in our players on the one hand and completely withdrawing from them on the other. While fostering dependency may produce some short-term benefits, it carries high risks for both player and coach over the long term. Remaining aloof from the players—a role we typically associate with the 'administrative coach'—may work in certain large team sports like major college and professional football, but it too carries risks, including a diminished understanding of the needs and motivations of the players."

Section Three

The World of Coaching

Staying Sane

In the first section of this book, we looked at the coach as an individual. In the second section, we broadened our perspective to include personal interactions with family and players. Now we'd like to broaden the perspective even more and look at the world of coaching in general. This where we will really get into the area we call The Other Stuff.

How many times have you complained, "If only I could just coach!" What you really mean is, "If only all this Other Stuff would stop interfering, I could really do a much better job teaching the players and managing game strategies." Well, the intrusions won't stop. For most coaches, time spent on the field is at least equaled by time spent on The Other Stuff.

Today, even the volunteer coach of a team of first-grade kids must deal with The Other Stuff. Coaches at all levels have to operate under some sort of hierarchy—a community board, supervisor, league president, parks and recreation official, athletic director—in other words, a boss. They must negotiate schedules, work within budgets, deal with parents, worry about injuries, deal with equipment and facilities—on and on and on.

Some coaches not only have to know and comply with the complex and ever-changing rules set forth by their own institution or organization, but also those set forth by state governing bodies, national sports institutions, and collegiate organizations such as the NCAA.

Some of the problems coaches encounter when dealing with The Other Stuff are manageable. A coach would have a realistic chance of dealing with them successfully. Others are less manageable; there's really not much that you as an individual coach can do to solve them. When faced with such a problem, you have several options:
- recognize your limitations and work within them,
- ignore the problem and risk organizational and legal violations,
- become so enraged at the problem that you spend more time trying to change the system than you do coaching, or

• give up in frustration.

We are going to ask you to take a good look at that first option if you want to survive and thrive as a coach. How can you recognize your limitations and work within them? We'll try to answer this question by beginning where we began the book—looking at you, the coach, as an individual.

Would you say that you are primarily externally or internally motivated? Externally motivated people allow things outside their control to define their behavior. Internally motivated people determine their actions from their internal sense of self. For example, an externally oriented athlete plays for the scouts and puts so much pressure on himself that his performance suffers. An externally oriented coach makes decisions based on how others might feel about her: "If I win the game, I'm a successful person."

Remember, it's not what you do, it's who you are as a person and how you do what you do. The internally oriented coach with a firm handle on his or her personal values and self-esteem is much less likely to get in trouble, burn out, quit, or be fired than one who defines himself or herself according to a job description.

You're Not Just a Coach

When you got into coaching, you looked forward to the challenge of working with a group of athletes and helping them to perform at the highest level possible. You observed other coaches conduct practices and manage games. You read up on the latest coaching techniques and theories. You may even have studied coaching in college. You thought you were prepared for whatever the job could hand you.

Then reality struck. On the first day of basketball practice, only seven of the twelve girls who'd enrolled in the program showed up at the community center. It turned out that the mother who was supposed to pick up the other five had to work late. So you, the brand-new volunteer coach, had to leave the seven at practice to go pick up the other five at home. Welcome to the job of chauffeur.

Very quickly, you found out that you were expected fill several roles for your players. You weren't just a coach, you were a social worker, substitute parent, therapist, medical advisor, and nutritionist. You were expected to perform all of these jobs in addition to guiding your team to a winning season.

Having a large staff doesn't diminish the number of jobs you're expected to perform, either. Some people think that major college programs have so many assistants and specialists that all the head coach has to do is manage, teach, and strategize. Well, he or she also has to deal with injury management, recruiting rules and windows, booster clubs, players who've violated rules, trip planning, drug testing, and—oh yes, helping all those assistants develop and grow as coaches.

When coaches say "the best time of the day is 2:30 p.m.," they mean that's the time they can go to practice and do what they once naively thought was the only thing coaches did—teach players how to play the game. That's really all most coaches want to do. They thrive on helping kids think, act, and feel better. No one ever warned them that this was just one of many jobs they would be expected to do.

What follows is a partial list of the jobs and duties that coaches are typically asked to handle. We are sure that you could add more items to this list.

MEDICAL SPECIALIST

Training, conditioning, and the treatment and rehabilitation of injuries are crucial components of any sports program. As a coach, you may need to interact with many different health professionals. These professionals usually have only the best interests of the players at heart. Sometimes, though, conflicts may arise between physical therapist and physician, physician and trainer, trainer and strength coach, strength coach and nutritionist, or even between members of the same discipline. You're the coach. Who makes the decision as to whether or not an athlete is ready to play?

JOHN:

"One of the main problems a coach faces is determining when an injured player can safely return to action. In community youth programs, it should be the responsibility of the parent and the child's doctor. In reality, though, the injured athlete doesn't always go to see a doctor, or the family doctor isn't as knowledgeable as he or she should be on sports medicine and athletic injuries. Lacking good advice, parents may take one extreme or another—either pulling their child out of the program altogether or pushing the child back into the game when he or she really isn't fit to play.

"However much coaches may wish it weren't the case, they often are the ones who must make the final decision about when an injured kid is fit to play. It's a difficult decision to make. Play a kid too soon, and you risk further injury and a possible lawsuit. Be too cautious, and you pointlessly deprive a kid of the benefits of athletic activity and hurt the team's chances of winning.

"Ideally, the association or league in which the team plays should have a written policy on injuries. Such policies are becoming more prevalent at all levels of competition because of the dangers of litigation, though not all organizations have them."

In high schools (as opposed to colleges), the health care providers working with the athletes are usually not part of a permanent staff but rather community practitioners working as independent contractors or volunteers, although there are certainly exceptions to this rule. Because the high school coach's relationship with such providers is more tenuous and less hierarchical, battles for structure can easily erupt.

Similarly, many athletes nowadays are hiring personal trainers, presenting coaches with yet another opportunity for a battle for structure. Coaches must have a clear set of their own rules and guidelines for conditioning and rehabilitation if they are going to withstand these battles. They need to have the confidence to stand up for their rules and guidelines in the face of a personal or community practitioner who might, for example, use a regimen of rigorous free weight training that is inappropriate for the age of the athlete or the particular sport involved.

RICK

"The complexity of big-time university programs can present its own special problems for coaches. In some cases, it's not the quantity of health care available that's the issue, it's the quality and appropriateness of that care.

"Consider the following example: A newly hired football coach brings his own orthopedic and sports medicine specialists with him when he takes over the program. The treatment philosophies of these specialists are very different from those already in place at the institution. The new coach says, 'You say you already have a sports medicine department at the university hospital? Fine. I'm sure it is quite good. But you hired me to win our conference and take the team to a major bowl game within three years. I need this medical team to accomplish that goal.' End of debate.

"This same coach brings his own strength and conditioning team with him. Two of these professionals are really coaches in disguise (see the subsection on 'normative cheating' below), and two are trainers whose experience and expertise is restricted to the

---

sport of football. So what does the tennis coach or the swimming coach or the soccer coach do now? The new trainers know nothing about strength and conditioning programs that are appropriate for tennis players, swimmers, or soccer players. But to make room for the two new football trainers, two other trainers with broader approaches to conditioning and strength training have been let go.

"Another difficult health issue in college sports—and in sports for both younger and older athletes, for that matter—is the issue of performance enhancement. Some performance-enhancing drugs, including anabolic steroids, are banned from all sports. Very few coaches today will risk becoming involved with steroids directly. But coaches often know who on their team has access to such drugs and who is exhibiting symptoms of steroid use. If these coaches don't intervene when they suspect steroid use, it is because they are more interested in short-term performance than in the long-term health of the kid. The issue has taken on even more importance today since Mark McGwire broke the record for home runs in a season. He freely admitted to taking a substance called androstenedione, which has been banned by many governing organizations, including the NCAA, but is legal in professional baseball. It is readily available as a 'nutritional supplement,' as is creatine, a similar amino acid-based supplement. You need to know about these types of supplements, both legal and illicit, because you are going to get asked about them by your players, administration, parents, and the media.

"Coaches need to be alert not only to the abuse of performance-enhancing drugs but to the abuse of recreational drugs as well. Coaches at all levels need to be knowledgeable about the signs of drug abuse and about the rules of their particular institution, organization, or association regarding intervention, parental notification, treatment options, punishment, and eligibility."

SURROGATE PARENT

Sometimes a coach must operate "in loco parentis." That doesn't mean the coach is crazy; it just means that the coach stands "in the place or position of a parent" in relation to a player. More and more today, coaches are asked to act as substitute parents for their athletes. And as any good parent will tell you, parenting is a full-time job. Unfortunately, not all coaches are prepared to take on the responsibility of teaching basic life skills to a player who should have already acquired such skills from his or her parents. Parenting skills are not taught in coaching classes or written about in coaching books. Even if the coach is a parent, working with another person's child is much different than working with your own.

RICK:

"What coaches are doing when they parent one of their players might more accurately be called 're-parenting.' In the past, it was just assumed that parents taught their kids the basic life skills that make up what psychologists call "emotional intelligence": how to be polite, to respect others, to clean up after yourself, to be responsible, to be empathetic. Today you have kids who don't seem to understand that it's not okay to steal, or to slap around your girlfriend. Or who lack such personal management skills as the ability to get up on time, keep a schedule, finish work, or turn in assignments.

"Society is relying more and more on institutions outside the family to teach these skills to kids. One of the institutions that is being asked to pick up the slack for parents is organized sports. Most coaches are much more involved in re-parenting their players than they ever anticipated they would be.

"Re-parenting consumes a great deal of time and energy, and it impacts coaches at every level of competition, from Little League to

---

the pros. When you see a pro star doing something highly inappropriate, you can be sure that the behavior didn't just appear all at once. The pro coach inherited the problem from the college coach, who got it from the high school coach, who got it from the youth league coach. Now the pro coach has to try to re-parent a guy making millions of dollars a year, who has the emotional intelligence of a child."

JOHN

"I was recently forced into the role of substitute parent during one of our summer camps. I noticed a boy about twelve years of age crying. He had hit the ball to the infield but hadn't run it out. That's one of our rules: you have to hustle and touch first base.

"I called the kid over to explain some of the basics of baseball to him. I wanted to tell him that he wasn't going to get a hit every time—that just putting the ball in play was an accomplishment in itself. But he wouldn't talk to me. He just sat at the end of the dugout, crying. Finally he stopped long enough for me to ask him what the problem was. 'I don't like to be yelled at,' he said. 'I wasn't yelling at you,' I replied. 'I just wanted to get your attention to talk to you.' He said, 'Well, one of the other coaches yelled at me. My dad hollers at me all the time at home and says he is going to beat me up.'

"Suddenly, I'm dealing with a very different and much more serious issue than I had anticipated. I asked the kid directly whether or not his father had physically beaten him. He was evasive, refusing to confirm that he had been physically abused, but it was obvious that, at the very least, he had been verbally abused and physically threatened. He was absolutely traumatized by any adult male yelling at him.

"The other coach who had been with the kid all through the week of camp was frustrated and annoyed. The kid wouldn't do anything he was told to do. The coach finally raised his voice. At that point the kid just fell apart. He only was in camp because his father wanted him to go.

"The kid thought that if he didn't get a hit every time, he was a horrible player. His father had reinforced a sense of inadequacy and low self-esteem in the boy. Now, I had to consider what I could do as a substitute father to try to repair the kid's self-esteem, at least to the extent that it affected his play on the field. First I coach the other coach on how to deal with the kid. I told him the boy had problems from outside the camp environment that we weren't going to solve in the two days remaining, to go easy on the kid and not raise his voice.

"Then I developed enough of a personal relationship with the boy to explain that even the best major leaguers didn't get on base every time and all I wanted from him was his commitment to run everything out and to have fun.

"I had to spend a lot of time off the field reparenting one kid—time I might have spent helping a whole bunch of kids with their fundamentals on the field."

FINANCE DIRECTOR

Many coaches are ill prepared to manage the finances and handle the budgets of contemporary sports programs. Yet, it is something they are often asked to do.

At the community program level, coaches are often expected to raise funds. Who is going to sponsor the team? Should "Joe's Bar & Grill" be printed on the uniform of ten-year-old athlete? Who can I put the arm on to sponsor a billboard? Can I sell enough ads to print the program?

Add in the requirements of today's sophisticated traveling teams, and a coach may have to be a banker and accountant as well as a fundraiser. Some independent club teams operate with larger budgets than those of small colleges. Junior-level hockey programs have permanent staffs, sophisticated booster clubs, and major marketing campaigns. The same is true of some soccer and basketball programs, as well as other sports.

At the club and high school level, a coach may be asked to be a financial advisor, too. When scouts approach a top club or high school player, a coach may find himself or herself sitting down with members of the player's family, helping them analyze their financial picture, and recommending the best next step for the player. The player's family may look to the coach for advice about how to get the maximum amount of aid for school or what college programs offer the most value relative to cost. The coach will need to educate the family about such things as the difference between partial and full scholarships and the long-term financial benefits of choosing one institution over another. The family will expect the coach to be straight with them.

University coaches have their own numbers games to manage. For example, they have to figure out how to divide a limited number of scholarships among a large number of players. Deciding who gets a full ride, who gets partial aid, and who gets left out for a year is a difficult and emotionally draining process. If you have promised a family that their son or daughter will receive a full scholarship and then don't deliver for some reason, you will not only have betrayed their trust, but you will be setting yourself up for any number of potential problems, from losing the player to being sued.

To illustrate some of these financial issues, let's consider the example of a young hockey player, whom we'll call Bill, who, as a Bantam, shows great promise. He comes from a good home, but his parents don't have a lot of money. First decision: Is he going to play for his neighborhood high school, for a nearby high school with dominant hockey program, for a private prep school in another state, or in a Junior hockey program several hundred miles away? The decision is really a financial one.

The local high school coach points out that they have a good, competitive program, and all of Bill's friends go to the school. He also points out that there are costs involved with any of the other options: travel, room and board, tuition (in the case of the private school), and all the incidental costs associated with going away from home.

The coach of another public high school in the same metropolitan area—a school with a hockey dynasty—emphasizes that, with the state's open enrollment policy, Bill can attend any high school he wants within certain guidelines. There will be no tuition; Bill can live at home. As for the commuting costs, well, the coach knows that Bill's mother is looking for a part-time job. He also knows that a booster of the program has a perfect position for her. Heck, Bill's mother might do so well that Bill can get his own car to make that commute. Just go see a local dealer who also is a booster.

The coach of an elite private boarding school in a neighboring state has a different pitch. He states that 92% of the graduates of his academy go on to college, most to top-flight universities. He also has scholarship funds that will pay for most of Bill's expenses. Bill can work for the school part-time to pay for what's left of Bill's expenses. Bill's educational experience at the private school will be far superior to any public school, the coach assures Bill's parents.

The Junior program that is recruiting Bill is in a state five hundred miles away. The assistant coach who has been following Bill knows all about his family. Bill's father is a hockey fanatic who played on semi-pro teams until he was over forty. He still plays on an "over thirty-five" team. The coach sells his program to Bill and his family purely from the point of view of playing hockey, telling them that no high school or prep school program offers the intense training and high level of competition that Junior hockey does. The costs to the family will be minimal. Bill will be given a stipend to cover his room and board, education, and incidental expenses. There are so many players on the team from Bill's home town that the program provides free transportation home for the players at the beginning and end of the season and at Thanksgiving and Christmas. If Bill were to enroll in the program, the coach argues, he is good enough to qualify for a full athletic scholarship at a university or to turn pro at the end of his Junior career.

RICK:

"Tough choices—for Bill and for his parents. The coaches make the decision difficult by playing up the advantages of each program. The two public high schools are the more economical choices, and their coaches both tout this fact to the recruit and his family. One of the coaches, however, goes further than the other to entice the athlete, practicing what is called "normative cheating"—that is, bending the rules without technically breaking them. The prep school and the Junior program tout the long-term benefits of joining their programs. The private school coach talks about the quality of the education at the school, the likelihood of Bill being accepted to an excellent college, and the monetary value of such an education whether or not Bill fulfills his hockey dreams. The other talks about Bill's enhanced market value to a big-time university program or to the pros.

"Using financial inducements to manipulate sixteen- and seventeen-year-olds and their families is becoming commonplace. It's even becoming common for younger athletes. Two of the larger athletic shoe manufacturers scout basketball players as early as eighth grade. The most promising players are 'signed up' by the companies. They are given several pair of $150 shoes. They receive bags, warm-ups, tee shirts, shorts, and socks, all with one or other of the famous logos of the two competing companies.

"In the summer, the companies run leagues for athletes fourteen years of age and up. No expense is spared on the quality of the facilities, equipment, or coaching. The coaches are hired by the shoe companies, and some make close to $100,000 per year. The best of the best players travel across the country, honing their skills, performing for college and pro coaches, and, unfortunately, developing a distorted and unrealistic view of life.

"Some high school programs are even signing contracts with the shoe companies. The high school coach is paid to require his team to use one or the other company's products exclusively. Star players who have gone through a shoe company's summer program are encouraged to transfer from their local school to a school that has contracted with that shoe company. The scouts and college coaches know good talent will be on display at these schools and will tend to watch more games of a shoe-sponsored school than a regular program. The kids are eager to attend, because if you're going to a 'shoe" school, you are more likely to get noticed. It's a similar situation with so-called 'area code tourneys' and with many Junior-level hockey teams.

"As the popularity of sports increases and the revenues generated by athletics continues to grow, more money is going to be coming to more players at younger and younger ages. Coaches need to be careful that their short-term interests don't blind them to the long-term needs of their players."

Once coaches begin to help players and their families understand and negotiate offers from scouts and agents, they are functioning in yet another role—as player representatives. While some rules have been relaxed to allow sports agents to become "advisors" to a player's family, a direct relationship with the amateur player is still problematic. An athlete good enough for the pros will naturally turn to his or her coach for guidance. Not that you as a coach need any more stress or responsibility put upon you, but it helps to be right up to the minute on your knowledge of both the rules of your institution or organization and the market value of athletes.

Some professional sports organizations, such as the NHL, allow a pro team to draft players and retain the rights to them even if they choose to attend or remain in college. Others, like Major League Baseball, set a time limit for rights. Whatever the sport, the kids are turning pro at younger and younger ages. What's your advice for your star? If you suggest staying in school and turning down the pro offer, how do you deal with the suspicions that you are acting in your own interest and not that of the kid? How do you determine what the best interests of the kid are?

If you are going to accept the responsibility of acting as a representative for your players, then you had better be prepared to keep a sharp eye on the actual sports agents. Most are ethical and would not do anything deliberately to jeopardize an amateur player's eligibility. But some would do just that—buy the kid a meal, some clothes, a pair of shoes—just to have leverage. If you want to have the most impact on your athletes in this area, you can counsel them about the ramifications of turning pro—how not every player who signs gets that million-dollar bonus or has a successful and lucrative pro career. You can also counsel them on how to handle themselves if approached by an agent so that they don't lock themselves into something they didn't intend or want to do.

Sometimes, coaches may find themselves taking on the duties of yet another financial advisor—the loan officer—in the sense that they must figure out how to arrange and secure a player's finances so that he or she can attend a specific program. Here's an example of what we mean. Let's say a good basketball player—call her Wendy—is being recruited by both the state university and an Ivy League institution. Wendy is a good student, interested in studying mechanical engineering, and has good entrance test scores—so she qualifies academically for either school. The decision of which school Wendy will attend, then, comes down to a question of finances.

The state university coach has a decided advantage here. She can offer Wendy a full scholarship and the opportunity, under the new NCAA rules, to work during the school year—and not just busy work, but career-advancing work for a famous local engineering company whose CEO is an alumnus and a member of the booster club.

How does the coach of the Ivy League school, with no athletic scholarships and with annual expenses for students in the tens of thousand of dollars, compete with this? She competes by knowing how to package the student's finances. Because she has a close working relationship with the admissions officers and the financial aid specialists and can generate a list of every academic scholarship opportunity, every grant, every prize, and every loan available to a person with Wendy's profile, she is able to whittle that twenty grand down to a number that still requires a heavy financial contribution by the parents but is low enough that the argument of "quality of education" has a chance of success.

Of course, the Ivy League coach goes home afterwards and lays awake most of the night thinking, "I just talked these folks into taking a second mortgage on their home so Wendy could come play for my program. What if she gets hurt? What if she just can't cut it at this level? The poor parents are still going to have to pay off that mortgage."

JOHN:

"Coaches of so-called 'nonrevenue' sports some-times have to know even more about finances than coaches of revenue-producing sports. For example, they may have to manage booster funds to meet regulatory and university guidelines. Or they may have to locate and acquire funds from outside their regular budget allocations in order to purchase new equipment or improve their facilities. I remember when I wanted to start a tour-nament to showcase our baseball team in competition with some of the best teams in the country. I wanted to hold the tournament early in the season at what was, then, the new indoor stadium in downtown Minneapolis. My athletic director told me, 'Sounds great, John, but you'll have to find the money on your own, because there is nothing budgeted for it right now.' I had to go out and search for a major sponsor. Luckily, I found one, and the tourna-ment is still going strong after more than a decade."

SOCIAL WORKER

Coaches become de facto social workers when they negotiate within the system to provide for their players an experience that is appropriate to their financial, cultural, educational, psychological, and social needs. In many ways, coaches are caseworkers, and their players and the players' families are their cases.

RICK:

"Every kid comes from a unique family situation. If you have twenty players on your team, you have twenty unique family situations. When these players have family problems, you, the coach, are often the person they go to for help and advice. You're supposed to have the answers to such problems as how to handle an abusive relationship, the death of loved one, or divorce. I know a situation where a women's basketball coach had two kids on the team who were pregnant. Does she play them? How does she counsel them when they ask tough questions about abortion?

"They don't teach you how to deal with this stuff in coaching school. But you're supposed to be there to handle it anyway.

"Some coaches are more adept at handling these types of situations than others. But I would caution all coaches against getting in over their heads. Pay attention to your gut feelings, and ask for help when you sense that you need it. It's tempting for coaches to try to solve problems beyond their training and end up causing more problems for the kid, for the others on the team, and for themselves than if they'd done nothing at all. Sometimes it's better to turn the kid over to an appropriate professional than attempt to solve everything yourself."

COP

A coach acting as a social worker can quickly find himself or herself being drawn into the role of cop when the problem the player is facing is something like substance abuse. You may be the only person a troubled player trusts, but you've probably had only a minimum of training in areas such as chemical dependency and the law. Your first responsibility is to convince the player to seek professional help. And, if legal or criminal issues are involved, you are also obligated to report what you know to the proper authorities. If you don't get the appropriate professionals and authorities involved, you risk damaging both the player and yourself.

JOHN:

"Coaches routinely act as cops to enforce team, school, association, and league rules. We've got rules on just about everything these days, but, for most school athletic programs, they break down into three main categories: cheating, drug use, and social contact. When the players are living away from home, the coach is made to feel that he or she is responsible for them twenty-four hours a day. Of course, kids never get into trouble during regular working hours. It's always in the middle of the night or on a weekend. The time I am most concerned about my players' behavior is spring break. At the University of Minnesota we schedule games over this period, so the players remain on campus. Outside of practice and games, there's not much for them to do, and so some have gotten into trouble in the past. Having to be 'always on duty' can create stress for a coach and cause friction between coach and family, coach and player, and coach and administration.

"At the University of Minnesota, regular mandatory seminars are conducted for the players on such subjects as sexual abuse, sexual harassment, and alcohol and drug abuse. The coaches have to make sure the players attend the seminars. The coaches also are required to enforce drug testing and to monitor the study table.

"When institutions insist on holding coaches responsible for the actions of their players, a coach's natural response is to tighten control of the athletes to prevent them from getting in trouble. The coach may dedicate a considerable amount of time to seminars and role-playing so that, if a kid does break the rules and get in trouble, the coach can say, 'Hey, it's not my fault. I did everything possible to prevent this.'"

RICK:

"Athletic departments have, at various times, asked me to function as a cop, but I have to say no. I could not maintain my credibility as a therapist with the players if they feared that I was spying on them or might report them for some minor infraction. When I was at the University of Wisconsin in Madison, I was asked to take charge of drug testing, and I refused. I would have been ineffective as a therapist if the players had perceived me as an arm of the campus police. It would have compromised my ability to establish a confidential, trusting relationship with the players."

POLITICIAN

Don't underestimate the importance of being a good politician. The youth sport coach who is adept at interacting with the governing board, the facilities managers, the schedulers, and the boosters is going to have a much easier time managing his or her program. The high school coach who gets along well with the school administration, league officials, parents groups, and the media is generally going to encounter fewer problems than a coach without good political skills, and enjoy more widespread support when problems do arise. Accommodating diverse interests and coordinating these interests toward focused, achievable goals is an important part of a coach's job.

The management of change, no matter how seemingly insignificant, involves politics. The team is only one part of a much larger system that the coach must work within. Just think of the things a coach may have to negotiate in any given season: schedules, rankings, sponsorships, equipment purchases, improvements in facilities, awards, travel, per diems, transportation, team photographs, rule changes, compensation, media coverage, publicity and promotion, parent conferences, staff training—the list goes on and on. Sometimes it takes all a coach's political skills just to keep his or her job.

Being a good politician increases your chances of winning the battle for structure—or at least of working out a compromise so you don't lose the battle.

JOHN:

"A major political issue for university coaches today is the continuing implementation of Title IX, the federal law preventing gender discrimination in college athletic programs. If you are the coach of a woman's sport, you want to make sure that your budgets, facilities, and pay are comparable to what the coaches of men's sports are receiving so that your female athletes have opportunities equal to male athletes. If you are the coach of a men's team, you want to advocate for the things your team needs to be competitive, while at the same time promoting the objectives of Title IX.

"Access to facilities is a case in point. At the University of Minnesota, the woman's softball coach and I worked together to gain access to the indoor football training facility on a regular basis so that our teams could practice inside during cold and inclement weather. We also agreed to share our respective outdoor fields during summer camps. It's all politics—working with others and reaching compromises that benefit all parties concerned as much as possible."

ACADEMIC ADVISOR

Academic performance off the field intersects with athletic performance on the field even at very young ages. For example, a volunteer coach for a youth soccer league is affected by academic performance when the parents of the team's star defensive player pull their daughter off the team after she fails math. Many coaches in a situation like this will shift into the role of academic advisor. The coach may choose to sit the player down and remind her of her priorities and commitments. Or she might recommend a competent tutor for the girl. Or, if the coach is familiar with the local school's math curriculum, she might help the player herself.

As the player progresses from traveling team to high school team to college team, the coach's role as academic advisor tends to become more formalized and more central to his or her job description, but coaches at all levels find themselves fulfilling the role of academic advisor, whether they're prepared for it or not.

JOHN:

"Coaches today are judged on more than just their win-loss record. The academic profile of the team is the coach's responsibility. Graduation rates, progress toward a degree, grade point average—there are incentives for meeting academic goals written into many college coaches' contracts.

"My mentor, Dick Siebert, was concerned about my academic performance when I pitched on his baseball team as a student at the University of Minnesota. He once told me, 'Anderson, you've got things backwards; your grade point average and your earned run average are reversed!'

"We didn't have an academic advisor for the baseball program back in the seventies. If a kid was failing, one of the coaches checked on him to make sure he was going to class and warned him that if his grades didn't improve he'd be kicked off the team."

"Today, the program does have an academic advisor. But if there is a problem, the coaches still have to resolve it. That can mean anything from talking with the player's instructors to expulsion from the team."

At major post-secondary institutions, the academic advising department acts as a buffer between the coaches and the instructors. At smaller colleges and high schools, the coach interfaces directly with the teacher when a player has academic problems.

If you must deal directly with faculty, it helps to be able to call upon some of those political skills we mentioned earlier. The more that you can do to subvert the stereotype that, because you're a coach, you don't care about academics, the more effective you'll be working with the player's teachers. You may also have to overcome the belief on the part of some teachers that the only time coaches come to see them is when they want a special favor for one of their star athletes.

Try to build some relationships with the faculty. Invite them to your practices or games; hold a special faculty day; take some faculty with you on a road trip. These sorts of bridge-building activities will help the teachers see that student-athletes are not just one-dimensional jocks— that they are, in fact, just like the instructor's other students. They will also help the instructors see that you honestly care about something other than your win-loss record.

RICK:

"Problems inevitably arise when coaches recruit athletes with serious academic problems or inadequacies. Take a small-squad sport like basketball, for example. Coaches at major colleges looking for a quick fix for their team often scout the junior colleges. But a junior college transfer may lack the academic skills and preparation necessary to succeed in a major college classroom. What happens to a coach's performance bonus, then, when the requirements to win a certain number of games and/or a conference championship collide with the requirements to maintain a certain team GPA?

"One last thought on this subject: It's important to keep in mind that the coach's primary agenda and the academic advisor's primary agenda are not identical. The coach is there to compete and to win games; the academic advisor is there to help kids get an education. The differing goals invite conflict and stress."

EQUIPMENT, FACILITIES, AND TRAVEL MANAGER

Not many coaches enjoy being an equipment manager. On the other hand, it's more than a little frustrating to show up for a competition and a player can't find his shoes. Coaches of young players are not the only ones who have to put up with this frustration. Any high school or college coach will tell you, older players can be just as forgetful as younger players.

Equipment problems, of course, aren't always the players' fault. Depending on the sport, any number of problems can occur: the balls aren't properly inflated, the nets aren't high enough, a hurdle is broken. Sometimes there isn't enough equipment on site to practice effectively or play a game. Although the coach is often given the responsibility for making sure there is adequate equipment and that the equipment meets playing regulations, many equipment problems are really problems with the system and are not within the control of single individual. For example, sometimes there isn't enough money to purchase new equipment. Or the process for ordering equipment is so complicated and bureaucratic, it isn't possible to have a purchase approved and the equipment delivered in time to use it. Or the institution or association doesn't have a contract with the vendor who carries the equipment you need.

A recent marketing strategy by major athletic apparel manufacturers has only added to the equipment-related problems coaches have to deal with. These manufacturers are enticing schools to sign exclusive contracts to represent their product. In return for having every team in the school wear the company's apparel, the company agrees to pay the school a generous amount of money—sometimes millions of dollars. One of the problems with such agreements is that no one company makes the best or most appropriate apparel for every sport. One company may make excellent running shoes but poor soccer shoes. Or vice versa. The soccer coach may be forced to use an inferior shoe unless he or she can get an exception to the policy, say by promising to wear every other part of the uniform from the contract company and to wear shoes from the other company with the logo painted over.

JOHN:
"While there are some positive aspects to exclusive equipment agreements, there are also some negative aspects, and these negative aspects can make life harder for coaches. For one thing, there's not a level playing field as far as the agreements are concerned. My team—and most of the teams in the Big Ten— have exclusive bat contracts. We get the bats for free. However, at least one team in the league doesn't have a bat contract so they must pay

for their bats out of their budget. With one aluminum bat costing about $350, the program without a contract is at a distinct disadvantage. If the coach can't put this into some kind of perspective, it's going to drive him crazy.

"Second, some players are joining college programs with arbitrary and unrealistic expectations about equipment deals. They have already had exclusive deals for years before they enter college and become annoyed if the college program has a different deal from theirs, or an agreement with (what they perceive to be) the wrong company. It's not easy to satisfy a kid who's been identified as a star and given free equipment, shoes, and clothes since he or she was thirteen years old."

Closely related to equipment management is facilities management. Managing facilities can frustrate coaches just as much as managing equipment. In youth sports, for example, everyone wants to use the same facilities at the same time: from 5:30 p.m. to 10:00 p.m. There's no place to practice because the facilities are being used for games. To practice, teams are forced to travel or to work out early in the morning or late at night—not the best of arrangements.

Many facilities aren't maintained as well as they should be. Instead of working with the players on fundamentals, coaches often find themselves spending large amounts of practice time fixing the field or wiping the floor or shoveling off the ice rink.

RICK:
"Sometimes a team doesn't have a place to practice, or the playing facility is bad and can't be used without major renovation. Many coaches have been put in the position of having to locate volunteers to help build a facility with their own sweat equity.

The facility may be satisfying to look back on years later, but constructing it takes a huge chunk out of the time that a coach should be using to teach his kids.

"I know one major university coach who felt his facilities were so bad he didn't schedule a home event for over five years. He weighed the relative disadvantages of always playing on the road against playing at home under horrible conditions and took what he felt was the lesser of the two evils."

The larger athletic programs have travel offices or dedicated agents to handle the logistics of moving large groups of people from one place to another. But, in most cases, if you're the coach, you're the travel manager, too. Even if you do have professional travel assistance, you are ultimately responsible for making sure all the travel arrangements work out right. Schedules change. Agents make mistakes. You have to check and recheck everything.

A youth coach who needs three minivans with volunteer drivers to take his or her basketball team to the game twenty-five miles away not only has to contact potential drivers who own minivans but also has to worry about arranging the pickup and drop-off points, checking for insurance, anticipating weather problems, and fixing the occasional flat tire. Even though travel planning demands an extraordinary amount of time, you really do want to plan for everything. There is an old military saying: "Proper prior planning prevents poor performance."

LAWYER

A coach who is not constantly aware of the legal ramifications of almost everything he or she does is likely to end up being called "defendant" rather than "coach."

RICK:

"An area fraught with the potential for legal problems is opposite-gender coaching: males coaching females, and females coaching males.

"In the fall of 1998, for example, North Carolina women's soccer coach Anson Dorrance, who had led the Tar Heels to fifteen national championships in seventeen years, was named in a twelve million dollar lawsuit by two former players who charged him with sexual harassment and other inappropriate conduct. The suit also named three other university employees, including Chancellor Michael Hooker.

"The plaintiffs sought one million dollars each in compensatory damages and a total of ten million dollars in punitive damages. They also sought a permanent injunction barring Dorrance from working with any athletic team or program where he would come in contact with female athletes or minors.

"Many current and former players and coaches came to Dorrance's defense. Several former UNC players said they hoped that when the case was concluded, Dorrance wouldn't change his coaching style. 'Coach Dorrance is a very demanding coach, but you need to be successful,' said Sonja Trojak France, a former UNC player and a third-year student in the Carolina medical school. 'He liked to know what was going on in our lives, but it was more about us being part of a team.'

"The suit is still pending, so there is no way to know whether or not the charges have any merit. But even if Dorrance were found innocent, his career has been seriously compromised. The case is another reminder that coaches must be continuously alert to how their words and actions may be perceived—or, in some cases, misperceived—by others. This is not to say that males shouldn't coach females, or vice versa; coaches should just be aware that such situations increase the potential for legal problems. And even though you are supposed to be innocent until proven guilty, the mere filing of a sexual abuse or harassment lawsuit can kill a career."

Sexual harassment is not the only legal issue that coaches need to be concerned about. More and more kids are charging their coaches with verbal abuse. Cultural attitudes about authority are changing, and the traditional drill sergeant approach to coaching that uses intimidation to discipline and motivate kids is going by the way. You are asking for trouble if you yell at your players. They will tell their parents and the parents will tell their lawyers and the lawyers will tell the administration and, before you know it, you will be the one being yelled at.

Physical contact of any kind with kids is always risky. Slapping a kid on the side of his helmet or grabbing a facemask might get his attention, but it also might land you in court for harassment or even assault and battery. Before you touch a kid, consider how your actions might be interpreted by others.

Lawsuits are expensive and they can end careers. One thing that you can do to prevent them is never to coach alone.

JOHN:
"In today's litigious climate, I strongly recommend having a witness around any time you discipline a player. If you are going to tell a player that you are terminating or reducing his or her financial aid, do it by the book and have a witness. Even when you make the original scholarship offer, it pays to have a witness.

"With the increase in lawsuits has come a corresponding

increase in the paperwork and procedures required for disciplining athletes.

"Let's say, for example, that you want to suspend a kid from the team because he or she did something you consider to be inappropriate. If you don't follow the proper procedures, you risk being suspended yourself. In almost all colleges and universities and in a rapidly growing number of high school and community programs, there are written guidelines for issuing warnings, providing counseling, signing contracts, and arranging mediation that must come in a particular order and be documented prior to suspension. You just don't kick a kid off the team unless there is a clear and eminent danger to the player or others on the team. Even then, be prepared to defend your actions."

There are any number of other areas that conceal potential legal land-mines for coaches, ranging from privacy issues to physical injuries. Indeed, the growing interest in sports medicine is at least partly fueled by litigation over sports-related injuries.

Don't let the fact that the modern world is sue-crazy drive you crazy. It's a fact. Deal with it. Protect yourself. Stay sane. Keep your job.

DIRECTOR OF OPERATIONS

Congratulations! You've just been named Head Coach. You have also just been named, whether you realize it or not, Director of Operations. The operations you direct may be as small as a youth hockey team or as large as a Division I football program. Size matters, but, in this case, not as much as you might think.

In a smaller program, as in a small business or single proprietorship, you will probably be doing most of the executive jobs yourself—

director of public relations, vice-president of sales and marketing, and chief financial officer, as well as president.

In a larger program, you will function more like a corporate chief executive officer. In a Division I football program, for example, there are executive vice presidents (offensive and defensive coordinators), line managers (position coaches), and staff functions (medical, training, human resources, academic counseling, information systems, sales, marketing and finance). Your job would be to direct the work of your staff to maximize the return on investment and increase shareholder satisfaction (which generally means going to a major bowl game).

To be a successful CEO, you need to know what's going on in all areas of the business. To gain that knowledge, you need be accessible. Get out of the office, circulate, check things out personally. The facilities assistant will be so thrilled that you took the time to speak with her, your playing field will be taken care of before those of the other head coaches. The travel office representative will be so happy that you treated him with respect, he won't hesitate to help you out the next time a flight is canceled, a hotel is full, or a bus doesn't show up.

As CEO, your jobs include managing staff development and training to make sure that all members of your management group are working together and at peak efficiency, and cooperating with the marketing department by speaking to booster clubs and attending other public events. You may also have your own television show—part of your executive compensation package. Sometimes the most successful head coaches in college and pro football know more about business management than they do about the Xs and Os. Who says sports is just a game?

>
>
> JOHN:
> "A business activity that most coaches are responsible for is raising funds. A youth coach tries to convince parents to pony up some extra dollars so the team can take a road trip. A high school coach lobbies a group of former players to kick in funds to renovate the softball field. A college head coach seeks support from booster clubs and other financial backers of the school. It helps to be a good fund-raiser at all levels of coaching.
>
> "Another business activity it helps to be good at is public relations. Some coaches have their own radio or television shows, and many more have regular contacts with the media, both print and electronic. The more adeptly coaches interact with the media and the public in general, the more effective they will be at raising awareness about their program and creating enthusiasm among fans. Increased awareness and enthusiasm can translate into increased gate receipts, advertising dollars, and community sponsorship. Of course, if the product (the team on the field) is consistently lousy, or if the coach has managed to alienate the consumers, no amount of PR or marketing will save his or her job."

Whatever the program, coaching is fundamentally a relationship business. If you treat others with respect, they generally will treat you with respect.

If you are a college coach, you will want to treat the high school and club coaches in your area with particular respect. Good coaches keep the best local prospects at home. Some coaches call it "building a wall around the state." If you don't plug yourself into the local coaching network, you are committing a major PR blunder. Visit the local sports clinics and summer camps. Assist area high schools with their major programs. Hold a scrimmage or preseason game in a part of the state that is not usually exposed to your program. If you don't schmooze with the local feeder network, you won't recruit the hot local prospects. It's that simple.

Success attracts attention. If you win games, the media will seek you out. Unfortunately, failure can sometimes attract even more attention. If (or rather, when) you have a serious crisis in your program, you won't be able to clear the reporters from your door with a fire hose. Normally, however, it's in a coach's best interest to seek out and cultivate members of the media. Remember the story of Jacques. Part of his successful battle for structure came when he made a friend of the local sports editor.

In addition to managing public relations, coaches must also manage human resources. Coaches manage human resources in several different ways. Recruiting is certainly a human resources-type function. Coaches, in essence, seek out and "hire" athletes to do certain jobs for them, just as corporate human resources managers head-hunt and hire employees. Sometimes coaches act as human resources managers for their players in a very different sense: They help their players find part-time or summer work (always being careful, of course, not to violate the rules of whatever body governs their conduct as coaches). In larger programs, this human resources function also extends into the hiring, promoting, and replacing of staff.

RICK:

"Part of a head coach's function is to manage turnover. Sometimes assistants stay with a program for many years and find career satisfaction in doing so. But most have a desire to advance into more responsible positions. You need to understand this and help your assistants achieve their career goals while getting the most you can from them while they are with your program.

"It's not easy to push an assistant out of the nest, but, if the assistant has stagnated in the job, he or she may need to move on. Encouraging that person to seek a new challenge is both good for the assistant and necessary for the continuing growth of the program. It's up to the head coach to recognize when both the program and the assistant would benefit from a change and to help the assistant make the move."

One executive job sets the head coach apart from all others on the staff. It doesn't matter whether the organization is huge or consists of one other part-time volunteer. The head coach is the crisis manager. To put it more bluntly: When Stuff happens, you're the one who has to plug the hole in the dike. You're the one who has to deal with the media or the administration or the staff or the players or the players' parents. It doesn't matter what the crisis is—the arrest of a player, a recruiting scandal, accusations of harassment, allegations of gambling. A crisis is a crisis. You're the boss. You must manage it. A good coach not only manages the crisis, but uses the crisis as an opportunity to educate staff and players.

TEACHER

One job most coaches actually look forward to taking on is that of teacher. Helping develop an athlete's skills, and then watching him or her execute is immensely satisfying and compensates for a great deal of The Other Stuff. In almost all sports and at all levels, there are opportunities for one-on-one instruction with talented young people who want to learn. Most coaches enjoy trying to discover what drives each player and using that knowledge to build the player's skills, confidence, and maturity.

There are really two kinds of teaching you do as a coach. You are aware of teaching the fundamentals and techniques of your sport. It's the other kind of teaching—the kind you do off as well as on the field—

that you may not be quite as aware of. But this second kind of teaching is just as important to the performance of your team and the development of your athletes and staff as the former.

RICK:

"We're always teaching something. We're just not always conscious of what that something is. We need to try to be conscious not only of what we intend to teach our kids, but what we actually do teach them. If there is a discrepancy between these two things, we are sending either mixed messages or the wrong messages. We need to continually examine ourselves to see if we truly are teaching what we want to teach.

"If we fly off the handle and act as if the world has just come apart every time the team loses, what are we teaching our players by our behavior? Anyone can get caught up in the moment—in the emotion of the game—but consistent behavior may send an unintended message to players, staff, fans, or the media.

"I once worked with a coach who had a volatile personality. During close games, he would stand on the bench and yell at the players and the refs. Once, when his team was trailing a traditional rival in a close game, the coach was throwing his usual tantrum, and I happened to look to the end of the bench where most of the freshman sat. They were all looking at the coach. You could see on their faces that they were thinking, 'You know, if coach is this upset, maybe things are really going in the toilet, and we should be scared, too.'

"A good coach is a good teacher, someone who has the ability to understand kids, believe in them, work with them, and keep them connected to the process. The good coach/teacher provides kids with plenty of opportunities to succeed so that they'll learn to believe in themselves and in the system."

Many coaches get angry when the kids "don't get it." In reality, the problem may be that the coaches don't get it: They haven't figured out how to communicate their message in a way that the kids will get it. Or the problem may be that the skill is unlearnable. To paraphrase Abraham Lincoln, "You can teach some of the skills to some of the players, and all of the skills to some of the players, but you can't teach all of the skills to all of the players." Just because you might be able to perform a particular skill doesn't mean your players can. This can be a problem with a new coach who formerly was a star athlete in his or her sport. If it was easy for this coach to shoot a free throw or make an accurate pass, he or she assumes it must be equally easy for the kids. You can never assume that skills are "easy" or "natural."

JOHN:

"We have a tendency to think we are good teachers because we had some success with one player or one team. When a new player or a new group doesn't get it, we think it must be because they are lazy or apathetic.

"Sometimes my staff will complain about guys making the same mistake over and over. I tell them that, while it's possible that the player lacks ability, it's also possible we haven't taught a skill effectively. We need to consider a different approach to teaching that skill. People learn in different ways and at different speeds. Maybe it's not the player's fault. Maybe the fault lies with us as teachers."

Some players combine natural athleticism with an ability to learn everything you teach them. Treasure these players, for they are a rare breed. Most kids fall somewhere along the spectrum from "great athlete, tough to teach" to "not the best physical assets, but really coachable." We always hear coaches complaining about what a bunch of fumble fingers they have this year or that this crop of kids is really empty between the ears. If you've been using these sorts of excuses, stop it! Even the pros have less than ideal players at some positions. You have to take what you have and get the most you can out of it. Now, are you a good teacher or not?

The coach who consistently gets the most out of the available talent is the one who varies his or her teaching methods to fit the kids rather than trying to fit square players into round positions.

But When Will I Have Time to Coach?

We've listed more than twenty jobs for which a coach is often responsible, in addition to running practice and managing games. You might not have personally handled all these jobs yet, but if you stay in coaching long enough you probably will.

So, when will you have time to coach? After all, you are primarily judged on the results of the team you put on the field. The coach who gets so wrapped up in all the other jobs and neglects to prepare the team probably should consider a career in administration. There are people who thrive on all The Other Stuff. We say, "Bless them!"

Everyone has strengths and weaknesses, likes and dislikes, when it comes to doing the jobs that coaches are asked to do. But whether you're good at them or not, or like them or not, the jobs still have to be done. You have to learn to manage your resources. Prioritize, delegate, do, or delay—whatever management strategy works for you. By being a good manager, you can make sure that all your duties are taken care of and still be able to coach the kids, have a life, stay sane, and stay in the game.

Complain, Blame, and Complain Some More

That's what a lot of coaches do. They complain about the unfairness of this or the inequality of that. They blame their problems on the weather or the administration or the kids or the government or the parents. Then they get together with colleagues and complain about the same things all over again.

One of the main reasons we wanted to write this book was to say to our fellow coaches, "Look, folks, we know all these issues and distractions are out there, but, for the most part, there isn't a heck of a lot you can do about them. The best thing you can do is learn to cope with these facts of life as positively and constructively as possible."

There is a distinct difference between standing up for what you believe in and committing career suicide. Complaining about systemic problems isn't going to make them go away. A coach who spends all his or her emotional energy fighting the system is going to have precious little left for coaching the team.

Sure, sometimes you need to fight. A supervisor may level a complaint against you or your program that is blatantly false. A governing body may establish a rule that is clearly antithetical to fair play. An association may ask you to use equipment that is dangerously unsafe. But understand that every battle has a cost. How much are you willing to pay? Who really wins and who really loses if you fight this battle? Is beating the system more important to you than coaching?

Many coaches have seen their careers derailed after they exhausted their emotional and professional capital fighting battles they probably shouldn't have become involved in in the first place. Pick your battles wisely. There is enough Other Stuff out there already to keep you busy. You can't stop the wind.

JOHN:

"I really try not to get upset with things that are totally out of my control. Some things I can control, and some things I can't control. I divide the things I can't control into two broad categories: acts of God and acts of government.

"Under acts of God go things like the weather. If you are a golf coach at a high school in Massachusetts, you are not going to have as much outdoor practice and match time as your colleagues from Alabama enjoy. What you can do to try to address this disadvantage is locate a dome to work out in during lousy weather in March and April and then thoroughly enjoy the pleasant days in May when your colleagues in the South will playing in ninety-five degree heat and ninety-five percent humidity.

"In early 1998, we took our baseball team to a tournament in San Diego primarily to take advantage of the superior weather there. Well, that was the year of El Niño. Three inches of rain fell and washed out the fields. We couldn't change it, so we coped with it. Dealing with this adversity made us a better team.

"Acts of government are almost as immutable as acts of God. Take Title IX, for example. I don't know of many employed coaches who still think women shouldn't have the same opportunities as men. I do, however, know some coaches who think that the implementation of the law has gone too far. But, coach, the law is not going to be repealed, so accept it, live with it."

Of course, it's one thing for us to tell you to accept your situation, and another for you to actually do it. There are some areas in particular that drive coaches nuts. We'd like to address three of those areas now in the hope that, by better understanding your problems, you can learn to make friends with them.

THE RECRUITING GAME

Earlier, we defined the concept of battle for structure and illustrated it with the story of Jacques, the hockey coach. If you are a coach involved in recruiting athletes, you've probably fought your own battles for structure recently. More and more, recruiting has become a battleground pitting player against coach. One of the problems is that the balance of power between kids and coaches is getting skewed. When a player asks, "What are you going to do for me?" or "How much are you going to give me?", he or she is putting the coach in a potentially compromising position. If the coach gives in to the player's demands during the recruiting process, the player's sense of entitlement increases, and more demands follow. If the coach doesn't give in, there is a risk that the player will sign with another program. The hard fact is that most coaches are capitulating to players' demands and are losing the battle for structure up front, before the relationship has had a real chance to develop.

Where do kids get this sense of entitlement? They get it from the media, who routinely trumpet stories about high school kids getting extravagant pro contract offers. They get it from other athletes who have gotten the star treatment themselves. They get it from high school and club coaches who imagine that they're big-time agents. They get it from parents who think their kid is the most talented athlete the world has ever seen.

RICK:
"If you need the kids more than they need you, you'd better not let them know it. If you do, you have lost the battle for structure even before the kid gets on campus, and you both will probably have a miserable experience.

"You have to learn to take a stand and risk losing a kid sometimes. I once heard an assistant coach tell a national recruit, 'There are a lot of reasons to choose a school: for the coach, for the education, for the relationships, for the tradition. If it's only about money for you, then perhaps we're not a good fit for you here, and you should go somewhere else. Why don't you consider our offer withdrawn?'

"That's defining what you want and what your program is all about. The word gets around when a coaching staff decides it's not going to let the kids run the program. The recruit in question signed with another school, lasted one year, transferred to another program, and then quit. The assistant coach who took the stand did so with the full knowledge and support of his boss. Both moved on to a bigger programs, and the assistant now is a successful head coach himself."

You're Not Recruiting a Kid, You're Recruiting a Family

There is a middle ground between caving into a kid's demands and withdrawing the offer entirely. Money and perks are rarely the only factors involved in a player's decision about which school to attend. The more knowledgeable you can become about the key influences and decision-makers in the kid's life, the better chances you have of winning the battle for structure and recruiting the player on satisfactory terms.

John:
"If you really want a kid, you have to get into his world. Take a page from the real gunslingers of our profession: the top football and basketball coaches in the country. They will tell you they find out everything they can about the kid and the kid's family, friends, community, hobbies, and interests.

"Before one of these coaches even begins to recruit a national player, they are going to try to use this information to give them a leg up on the competition. The coach will know everything about the recruit's world, including such details as what recreational activities the kid's family participates in, what church the family goes to, what jobs the parents hold and what unions, professional societies, or social organizations they're members of, where they take their vacations, and so on.

"The top recruiters gather all this intimate information to become part of the prospect's network—to join his or her system. Once they've done that, they can use the network to help them land the kid.

"Sometimes you learn that the family may be a liability to the kid's development in your program. You may not want the family closely involved. But at least you have information that can help you counter some of the kid's more unreasonable demands. Information helps you win the battle not only to get the kid in your program in the first place but to keep him or her there. Understanding the kid's background and family dynamics helps you individualize your coaching to that kid's needs."

There are a couple of other aspects of recruiting we should mention, one of which we touched on earlier when we discussed public relations and coaching, and that is the importance of forming good relationships with local and regional coaches. Too many coaches move into a new assignment in a new area and either badmouth the local programs or ignore them. Once this mistake is made, it can take years to make things right.

You need good relationships with local coaches to recruit effectively. The smart coach will build relationships so other coaches will recommend your program to their best athletes. It's really a larger battle for structure, and you've got to be smart about it. You need to build alliances with the high school and club coaches. You need these people. You have to work with them, become involved in their networks. If not, forget about recruiting home-state athletes.

Finally, we want to say something briefly about the recruitment of foreign players. "Foreign" can mean different things in different contexts, but we're referring specifically to the recruiting of players from another country.

No one denies that recruiting foreign players can bring very quick results. Many universities have improved their track and field programs overnight by importing a few national-class runners from other countries. The fame of the great Olympic distance runners from the high countries of East Africa attracts American recruiters, as does the outstanding baseball talent in Latin America.

Some coaches don't stop at recruiting a few national-class athletes, however. They import entire teams. It's a good deal for the coach. He or she gets an instant team of high caliber. It's a good deal for the members of the foreign team. They not only get to train in another country with top facilities, but they get an excellent education as well. So who isn't it a good deal for? Perhaps the good local player who had her heart set on playing for her state school and isn't even recruited. Or the high school or club coaches whose contracts require them to place a certain number of kids in Division I programs. They certainly aren't thrilled at seeing their stars lose scholarships to players from abroad. It bears repeating: local coaches have long memories. Something else we mentioned earlier applies here also: The further you go to recruit, the less you know about the kid and the family. You can't make too many home visits to Australia under the budget constraints of most programs.

There is no absolute right or wrong in recruiting foreign players. But it's worth asking yourself what's good for the kid as well as what's good for your program.

THE RATINGS GAME

It used to be only television shows got canceled because of poor ratings. But ratings mania has spread throughout the sports world and has changed the way many coaches are judged.

Ratings programs such as the Sears Director's Cup are having a profound influence on collegiate sports and college coaches. The Sears Cup is awarded annually to the school with the most combined points from all sports, men's and women's, revenue and nonrevenue. Points are awarded only if a school goes to an NCAA tournament. The farther you go in the tournament, the more points. There are other ratings programs, too. Some larger conferences like the Big Ten, for example, have initiated their own ratings systems.

It used to be that coaches of nonrevenue sports were only asked to run clean programs and graduate their players. Now, because of the new ratings programs, coaches of sports from fencing to softball to swimming have performance clauses written into their contracts. Winning means more because it potentially contributes ratings points. Coaches of smaller, nonrevenue programs are now being fired for performance reasons, just like coaches of revenue sports.

JOHN:

"In the last couple of years, many of the nonrevenue sports at the University of Minnesota have had very successful seasons. In fact, in the most recent academic year, the University ranked first in the Big Ten in combined points for all sports.

"Not long ago, a couple of coaches and I were visiting with a university administrator who congratulated us, then turned to the one coach among us whose team hadn't gone to an NCAA tournament and said half-jokingly, 'Well, coach, I guess we'll be looking to you for points next season. The rest of us can

---

coast!' We laughed, but I'm sure it was the first time that a coach of that particular sport was under an even implied pressure to win. Realistically, some programs just can't compete with others because of factors outside the coach's control. Being pressured to compete successfully against these programs in order to earn points can be very stressful."

DEALING WITH YOUR ADMINISTRATION.

A consistent problem in organized sports is the lack of strong leadership from above—the lack of clear organizational goals. Just as teams struggle under a coach who has no clear vision or direction, coaches struggle with mixed messages from athletic boards and directors.

Administrators tell the public, "Educating the kids is our primary concern," while at the same time they're saying to the coach, "If you don't win, you're fired." Such contradictory messages create enormous stress for coaches, putting them into situations where they're damned if they do and damned if they don't.

It doesn't matter so much what the specific organizational goals are as it does that they exist, that they are coherent, that they are communicated consistently both within and without the organization, and that the administration is uniformly committed to the goals. When this is the case, coaches can at least determine for themselves if they want to stay and work toward fulfilling the organization's mission or go somewhere else where the goals of the program and the coach are more closely aligned.

If your administration is sending you mixed messages and you can't influence those who control the program to give you a clear statement of mission, then about the best you can do, should you decide to stay in the program, is to become more internally oriented and figure how to get what you want out of the program. If you want to be a reformist, then go ahead—be a reformist. But if you just want to coach kids, then coach and don't let yourself get completely wrapped up in the politics. Don't form committees to protest this or that. That's not coaching, that's political activism.

RICK:

"Sometimes, we don't get mixed messages from the administration; we get no messages at all. As a coach, you may feel that your boss just doesn't care. That may or may not be the case. If you decide not to watch the performance of a player you've already recruited or not to go over and over game film because you have other more important things to do, your assistants or players may perceive that you don't care. Of course you care. You've just made an executive decision about your priorities.

"The same thing happens at the administrative level. It may look from the coach's position that the administrator doesn't care. But it's possible that the administrator has other, more important things to deal with. If an administrator is working to win a three-million-dollar grant from the state for the athletic department, the problem of one coach in one program may not be a high priority.

"Administrators are constantly setting priorities and making decisions that coaches are not aware of, the same way that coaches set priorities and make decisions without always informing players and staff. All of us think our particular problems are important, and we want them taken care of immediately. That's our focus and concern. It's hard sometimes for us to take a broader perspective.

"Later in the book we will discuss the loneliness of the head coach. But think for a moment about the typical athletic director. Talk about loneliness. Few people appreciate the isolation they feel, the pressures they're under, the problems they have to deal with. As coaches, we tend to rely on the athletic director to support us, and we feel let down when he or she is unavailable. The typical athletic director sits in the middle between administration and the individual coaches and programs. They get pressured from both sides."

JOHN:

"Sometimes we don't think the administrators are interested in our problems. But then we rarely take the time to go and talk to them. If we sought out our athletic directors more often, we might find out that they are more responsive and accountable than we imagined.

"When coaches don't seek communication and feedback from their supervisors, they're playing the old 'assume' game again. Administrators may just need to have an issue presented to them directly in order to take action. They can't help if they don't know.

"Let's face it, though, sometimes you're just a nuisance! A big time athletic program is not about the soccer team or the gymnastics team or the golf team. It's about football and basketball, which means it's about revenue. And it's about compliance, which also comes down to revenue. And it's about gender equity, which is also a revenue issue.

"Does that mean a coach of a nonrevenue sport can't have success and enjoy his or her job? No, not if you understand the reality of your situation. Your program isn't going to get as much support and attention from the administration as the football or basketball program, but you still can run a good program. You may have to do some fundraising on your own, but that's better than asking for the impossible from the department and then being frustrated when nothing happens."

Normative Cheating

No, we aren't saying that cheating is normal. "Normative cheating" was a term first used by Professor James H. Frey, now dean of the College of Liberal Arts at the University of Nevada–Las Vegas. He defined normative cheating as "strategies that are necessary to meet the goals of winning and are brought on by stresses that accompany the goals." These strategies are used by some of the top coaches and programs in the nation. They don't break the rules, and they would sue you for slander if you suggested it. They are, however, masters at pushing the envelope, at using loopholes and fine points to gain a competitive advantage.

In a paper titled "Deviance of Organizational Sub-units: The Case of College Athletic Departments" published in the *Journal of Sport and Social Issues* in May 1994, Professor Frey discussed what causes normative cheating:

> *Structural conditions in the form of barriers to success (for example: academic progress requirements) produce stress within the organization. As a result, the participation in deviant behavior can be a mechanism to reduce structural strain or to solve organizational problems associated with goal achievement. Factors such as the pressure for high performance (winning, post-season appearances, top 20), seemingly inappropriate legal requirements (NCAA regulations on the length of socks or the amount of money a player can receive for living expenses), a high level of competition from similar organizations, financial pressures, and uncertain financial resources can stimulate an organization to engage in deviant behavior.*
>
> *Gross (1978) asserts that deviance is likely to occur whenever individuals are placed in a position where performance is emphasized.... Clearly, the prospect of deviance is great when the coalition that pro-*

vides the resources expects programs to be successful even in the face of rising costs and deficit budgets.

Eitzen (1988) states that the culture of some sports promotes deviance, not fairness: "Getting such a competitive edge unfairly is viewed by many in these sports as 'strategy' rather than cheating."

In a nutshell, normative cheating is a strategy used by some coaches to reduce the stress caused by The Other Stuff. If a coach is under intense pressure to win (as most coaches are) and there are either rational rules (mandatory class attendance) or irrational rules (maximum length of socks) that stand in the way, that coach will be tempted to try to find a way around the stress-creating situation without breaking the letter of the law.

It's difficult to give precise examples of normative cheating, because what might be technically within the rules today will, if exploited enough, be against the rules tomorrow. So the practitioners of normative cheating are constantly shifting between the cracks in the rules. Here are three examples:

- The most popular course for freshman athletes at a prominent university is Portuguese. Why? Since few if any students have studied Portuguese in high school, the athlete is probably not competing against students with higher levels of knowledge. The athlete, therefore, is less likely to get a bad grade.
- In certain sports there are limits placed on the number of preseason competitions, and in all sports there are stringent regulations governing recruiting, so to get around these restrictions some colleges will schedule preseason "workouts" against the very best sixteen- to eighteen-year-old club teams in neighboring states. These scrimmages, conducted under full game conditions, don't count as "competitions" but do allow the sponsoring coach to try out the best high

school players without violating the "no tryouts" rule. At the same time the coach gets to show off the campus and the program without it counting as an official visit.

- There's a rule that says you can't send newspaper clippings to recruits. It was probably made so big programs with lots of press wouldn't overwhelm a recruit with big scrapbooks of clippings. What you can do, though, is send a letter to a kid and have copies of the clippings on the back. That, of course, is what many coaches do. There may be only one sentence on the front of the letter, but the practice does not technically violate the law.

When the NCAA creates rules, normative cheaters find ways to get around them. For example, the NCAA had a rule that you could only provide your athletes with one free meal a day. The rule defined a meal as food served in a food service facility. Several football programs got around the rule by having microwaves and commercial refrigerators installed in the weight room. The weight room wasn't a food service facility, it was a training facility. It really didn't serve meals; it provided nutritional supplements. This use of normative cheating allowed the program to serve free food around the clock.

Consider what an advantage this would be for recruiting. A prospect visits a school with such a "training" program and then comes to another school in the same conference and asks, "Where's the food?" If the second institution is obeying the spirit of the rule, they are immediately at a competitive disadvantage in landing the prospect.

The issue of financial aid is another area that invites normative cheating. Private schools like Miami, Duke, Northwestern, and Stanford have a tough time competing for recruits because of their higher tuition cost. However, they do enjoy an advantage over public schools, because they historically offer more "institutional" or "general" scholarships than do public schools. They can offer greater amounts of overall financial aid to a prospect to compensate for the higher tuition. It is another example of normative cheating, but it is doubtful the schools in question define it as such.

In a few southern states, lottery proceeds are used to guarantee any student of the state with a 3.0 high school average a tuition waiver to the state school. It's tough enough for a school in New Jersey to grab a top Florida recruit, but, with this program, the Florida coach could expend much less scholarship money and still give the recruit a full ride.

Rules limiting the number of coaches a sport may have can be subverted by normative cheating. Some big-time football programs get around the rules by adding "strength coaches" to their staff. These personnel are technically assigned under "strength and conditioning," and don't count against the number of coaches. The fact that one strength coach might be a wiz at teaching linebacker play and another was an All-Pro place kicker is mere coincidence.

Performance enhancement is yet another area where normative cheating thrives. While few coaches would risk their careers by permitting their athletes to use steroids, substances such as creatine and androstenedione do pretty much the same thing. Both are natural substances that aid in the development of body mass and strength. Androstenedione is a steroid that has been banned by many individual sport governing bodies and by the NCAA but not, as of the writing of this book, by all sports. Creatine is billed as a nutritional supplement and is not presently banned by any governing body. The use of either, even when allowed by the rules, is another example of normative cheating.

JOHN:

"In some college sports, a scholarship athlete can make one transfer without sitting out a year as long as he or she is given a release from the obligations of their scholarship by the original institution. This leads to situations where players are 'traded' almost like in the pros.

"Say, for example, that a college baseball program has recruited too many right-hand hitting infielders. A coach who practices normative cheating might say to one of his kids, 'Look, Joe, it's clear you aren't going to get much playing time here. Certainly not as much as you thought you would when you signed for the grant-in-aid. While we will honor the terms of our scholarship commitment to you, we just aren't going to be able to play you as much as you'd like. But, you know, I was talking to Coach Jones at our meetings last week, and he told me that he really needed someone like you. Why, I bet you could even start for him. If you want, I'll give you permission to go talk to him, and we will work on getting you a release from your obligations to us.'

"It is entirely a coincidence, of course, that Coach Jones has one catcher too many and that Joe's coach is short at that position.

"Legal? Yes, but right on the edge. Ethical? Very questionable. Normative cheating? Absolutely."

Even the high schools are getting into normative cheating. Since open enrollment became the law in many states, programs are competing against each other for stars with offers of weekend and summer jobs, deals on shoes, athletic gear, and even cars. Many coaches who are forbidden by the rules to work directly with the kids until a certain date encourage "captain's practices." A helpful parent or student videotapes the practice for later review by the coach, who gives the captains their agenda for the next practice when he just happens to run into them the next day at school. Some prep programs are notorious for their abuse of the practice of hiring "coaching interns," who normally don't count against the maximum allowable number of coaches.

Even programs for physically and mentally challenged athletes are exploited by normative cheaters. These sports leagues enable young men and women to play competitive sports under conditions in which alternative skills and desire more than compensate for severe handicaps. Some coaches, in their desire to win at all costs, are enrolling players with asthma on the physically handicapped teams. When challenged, they appeal. When denied, they slip the next ringer in. You have to wonder, a) should these folks be coaching kids at all? and, b) where is the line between what we are calling normative cheating and just plain old-fashioned cheating?

Over time normative cheating can become just another accepted practice. The recruitment of international students and junior college transfers to college programs is a good example. Recruiting techniques that once tested the limits of eligibility rules are now considered legitimate, mainstream practices.

RICK:

"Complying with the rules is a headache for coaches even under the best conditions. It's tough to comply with regulations that get more complicated with each successive season. (Of course, one of the reasons rules have to be so complicated is that normative cheaters keep opening up loopholes. As people find ways to circumvent the rules, new rules have to be written to stop them.)

"In reality, we don't all play by the same rules. If you as a coach

---

are competing against schools who push the spirit of the law, you are going to be at a competitive disadvantage. One solution is simply to say, 'We aren't going to push the limits of the rules as much as school X, and we may not get certain recruits because of it. That's who we are, and, as coach, I accept who we are.' This attitude is fine as long as you are supported by your administration. However, if your job is on the line, you may have no choice but to push the spirit of the law yourself. You want to be sure, though, that you keep in mind who you are, what your program's mission is, and why you're doing what you're doing so that you don't step over the line and do something you may later regret.

"Without a strong mission and clear goals for your program, you may find that the path of normative cheating leads you in directions you don't really want to go. When this happens, external factors tend to take control of your program and dictate your behavior. The only sure way to preserve your sanity is to keep focused as much as possible on your internal sense of self and to set goals that are realistic for your situation.

"Nobody ever said life was fair. But just because the playing field isn't level doesn't mean you can't keep a level head. Don't base your sense of self on how others define you; decide for yourself what's important. Once you've decided what's important for you, share your vision with your players, staff, administration, and others. Tell them, 'It doesn't matter how other schools are doing it. This is how we're going to do it here.'"

Remember the Kids?

Sometimes The Other Stuff can overwhelm us and we forget the real reason we're in this game.

A high school coach tells the story of how her principal started getting complaints from kids that the bathrooms were locked in the afternoons. The principal checked and found the complaints valid. He then went to the custodian and asked, "Did you lock the bathrooms?"

The custodian answered, "Yeah."

Perplexed, the principal demanded an explanation.

"Well," said the custodian, "I clean 'em at 1:30 and then I lock 'em so they don't get dirty again."

The principal said, "Yes, but school doesn't get out until 3:30."

"But then I'd just have to clean 'em all over again," the custodian replied in a self-righteous tone.

The principal reminded the custodian of the only purpose for having a school: "We're here for the kids. No kids, no school. No school, no need for a custodian or a principal. They're the only reason we're here at all, so you will clean the bathrooms after they leave."

As a coach, you have to remember why you are in the business.

ARE YOU THERE TO FULFILL YOUR NEEDS OR THE KIDS'?

The kids aren't there for the coaches' sake; the coaches are there for the kids' sake. Athletic program shouldn't be designed for the coaches; they should be designed for the kids. It's okay for a coach to be competitive, to want to advance his or her career, but a coach's primary purpose is to ensure that kids' experiences in sports are positive. If the kids aren't having fun, if they're not enjoying what they're doing, you won't be around long enough to have a career. Think about it.

JOHN:

"Too often, youth programs are set up for the convenience of the coaches and the 'system.' It's easier to play more games than to run an effective practice program in which the kids can develop their skills. Just throw them out there, and if they don't play well, it's their fault.

"At clinics, youth coaches tell us that they can't practice because there are no fields available. Well, the reason there are no fields is because everyone is playing games. Cut the number of games, and there would be an adequate supply of practice fields.

"Many communities are wrestling with the future of their youth sport programs. Such self-examination is productive if it leads to a set of objectives that are kid-centered and that emphasize process over results. We don't do a very good job of teaching process anymore, we've become so results oriented. Especially for younger players, the season should be a time of learning and skills development rather than a succession of competitive games. We need to be at least as concerned with the quality of play—that kids play well, play hard, play fair, and, most of all, have fun—as with winning games."

In order to be an effective coach, you have to get the kids to believe in your system. To do that, you have to give them opportunities to succeed. Once kids experience success under you, you become a credible leader in their eyes.

Part of being credible is formulating realistic expectations for players. The very best free throw shooter misses at least ten percent of the time. To set a goal of hitting every free throw would be unrealistic for any player. Setting unrealistic goals means setting kids up to fail.

What's Good for the Kid vs. What's Good for Business

John:

"We hear a lot these days about coaching kids 'from the neck up.' What people usually mean by this is teaching the kids discipline, poise, control, and emotional stability. This is getting to be a tougher and tougher job.

"One reason it's getting tougher is the changing nature of youth sports. Good athletes are told at a very early age that they have to specialize in one sport. They can't just be kids and try a bunch of different things in and out of athletics. If they want to be a good football player, they're told, they have to concentrate on football. If they want to be a good swimmer, they have to swim and nothing else. That means year-round, specialized weight training, beginning (in my opinion, at least) at too early an age. It means summer camp. It means winter conditioning. These young athletes are allowed to play other sports only to improve their skills for their main sport. By the time they enter junior high or middle school, they've not only been slotted into a specialized sport, but into a specialized position within that sport.

"By the time we recruit these athletes at the university level, they've developed unreasonably high expectations. They've been told by everyone at every level how good they are—all-state, all-American, all-everything. The fact that we're recruiting these players only confirms their exalted status.

"Part of our 'de-recruiting' process is to work with athletes on managing reality. We try to make them understand how difficult it's going to be to play at the college level. We explain that learning is a process and we don't expect them to do everything right away. Sometimes that works."

RICK:

"And sometimes it doesn't work.

"One of the things I don't think we do a very good job of is dealing with the fallout, the residue of specialization in sports. Everyone wants these highly talented kids to play, play, play, except, eventually, the kids themselves. They have been pushed and pulled and prodded and coerced for so long they've burned out.

"Suddenly, the most talented kid on your team isn't motivated to play. How do you, the coach, deal with this? You busted your tail to recruit the player, and now he or she won't perform. If you can't motivate the kid—and in many cases you can't—you may have to expel the player you most wanted on your team. This kind of stuff can drive a coach crazy.

"When athletes stop and ask, 'Why am I playing?' that's the time they need help. The question can be asked at any stage of a player's career, from youth leagues through the pros. The trigger can be an injury, declining performance, or burnout. Whatever the reason, the dependencies that many programs foster in top athletes may make it difficult for them to answer this question on their own. During therapy, we guide the kids to decide for themselves what they want, as opposed to most of their life in sports when they've been told by others what they want. We ask them to define what it is they want and need. We encourage them to be proactive rather than reactive.

"If we can get the kids playing because they want to, we know that they are more likely to perform at their best for longer periods of time than if they're playing because other people want them to. Kids' chances of achieving their potential increase as they take more active control of their own lives. And the nice thing for the coach is, you don't have to spend all your time taking care of them."

Section Four

Reality

Getting Unstuck

We've spent a good deal of the book so far looking at the various situations that affect a person's ability to survive and to thrive in coaching. In this section, we will use our experience with the University of Minnesota baseball program to take a look at a real program with real problems.

In 1994, John began to feel dissatisfied with the way things were going with the University of Minnesota baseball program. The program had stalled, and John wasn't sure why this was the case or how to push it to the next level.

John didn't understand that he was part of the problem.

THE HEAD COACH

John Anderson entered coaching with no formal training. He'd grown up in a small mining town in northern Minnesota, where he had been a good multi-sport athlete. After graduation, he'd come to the university as a JV pitcher with no promises and no scholarship. In retrospect, a shoulder injury that ended his hopes of being a successful pitcher in a big-time Division I program may have been a blessing in disguise. John became a student assistant for the baseball Gophers under Hall of Fame coach Dick Siebert.

John watched and learned as Siebert guided the 1977 University of Minnesota team to the College World Series. Twelve players from that team went on to sign pro contracts, including future Hall of Famer Paul Molitor. The high point of the year for John was when the players named him—the non-player, the student assistant—team MVP. John graduated in December 1977 with the intention of someday becoming a high school baseball coach. That would never happen.

Dick Siebert asked John to stay on as a graduate assistant coach during the spring season of 1978. When the season ended, John returned to his hometown and took a job working with a mining company. In late summer, Siebert asked John if he would assist him one more year for a stipend of about $4,000. Naturally, John, who was making over $20,000 in the mining job, quit, packed up his belongings, and moved back to the Twin Cities. Shortly afterwards, Siebert became extremely ill. He died in December 1978. John stayed on as an assistant to Siebert's successor, George Thomas, before being named head coach in 1981 at the age of twenty-six.

Thirteen years later, the baseball program appeared to be doing just fine under John's leadership. Over the years, he had guided his teams to several Big Ten titles and NCAA appearances. His teams had always finished first or second in the Big Ten, and he had never had a losing season, in the conference or overall. His 1994 team had won forty-two games and gone to the NCAA regional tournament.

All, however, was not what it seemed. Dissension was spreading among the staff, and even the players were becoming infected. Before too long, it would be necessary to call in a "head-head coach" to help diagnose and cure the problem.

THE HEAD–HEAD COACH

Like John, Rick Aberman also has roots in Minnesota, having grown up in the Twin Cities area. Instead of the University of Minnesota, though, Rick attended college at the University of Wisconsin, Madison, eventually becoming a member of the Badger's sports medicine staff. With his creed, "Decide what you want, then do it," he found true satisfaction and much success in helping players and coaches define themselves by who they are as people rather than by what they accomplish in athletics.

In the late 1980s, the budgets of the Badger athletic department were cut and five varsity sports were eliminated. Rick helped both coaches and players cope with the cutbacks. After his own position was eliminated, Rick began consulting with the Minnesota men's hockey and baseball programs in 1992.

Rick:

"After working with the University of Minnesota baseball program for a couple of years, I could see that a storm was brewing, but it hadn't progressed to the point where real change could occur. Things just weren't bad enough for John yet. The worst thing I could have done was to impose myself on people who weren't ready to work on their problems.

"It's like the old joke: How many shrinks does it take to change a light bulb?

"One—but the bulb must really want to change."

The Downhill Slide

Honest self-examination is difficult, but it's something coaches need to do to survive and thrive in the game. It doesn't matter whether you have a winning record or losing record, a new program or one steeped in tradition. If you sense that something is wrong, if you're uncomfortable with your situation, if you feel that you could be doing better, then you need to take a long, hard look at yourself and your situation.

John:

"Every once in a while, you have to step outside of your narrow everyday world and look at things from a different perspective. For example, when I coached the USA team in 1993, I was able to step out of my world at the university and gained a new perspective by watching how others did things.

"After the NCAA regional in 1994, I really felt that I needed a new perspective. The team had had a great opportunity to take the "next step," but we did not make it to the championship game. It was clear to me that I had not yet taught the kids how to control their emotions and play with relaxed confidence. Whenever they'd face adversity, they would lose control and stop playing as a team. At the time, I didn't want to deal with the problem head-on. I would rationalize our losses with the pat observation that the other guys were just better than us, when that often wasn't the case.

"But now I realize that the kids would panic and lose control when things got tough because the coaches were panicking and losing control. They would see us tighten up, and they would tighten up, too. A guy who hadn't made an error all year would suddenly let two balls go through his legs—that sort of thing.

"I wanted to find excuses for what was going on—these things 'just happen' or 'we were unlucky today' or 'it's too bad Joe had a bad game.' I ignored a whole bunch of warning signs and just stuck my head in the sand."

RICK:

"For anyone who's been around coaching for a while, there are familiar themes here. John recognizes that he has a problem, but he has no idea how to fix it. Let's face it, it's easier to push problems aside when you are winning and going to postseason tournaments than when you have just gone through a losing season and everyone is screaming for your head."

In the 1995 season, the team won enough games to return to the Big Ten tournament, and John thought that maybe his problems had been fixed or had simply gone away. That hope evaporated along with big leads in two tournament games. Once again the team reached a certain level and then stalled. They had a chance to win a big game, but experienced an almost identical breakdown to the one that had ended the previous season. John walked away from the tournament shaken, saying to himself, "You know what, there is a problem. It's not just that the other teams have better players. We're not getting the job done."

While John's uneasiness had developed into a real concern, the program's winning ways continued to mask the problems. While the team's performance at that Big Ten tournament had been painful for John, Rick still didn't feel that things had progressed to the point where John was ready for truly serious self-examination.

JOHN:

"I intended to address the problem in the summer of '95, but, as usual, I got bogged down in all The Other Stuff. Before I knew it, school had begun, it was time for fall practice, and I had resolved nothing.

"Instead of dealing with the problem directly, I was still looking for excuses and things to blame. If the players just tried harder, I told myself, the team would improve. If we did more conditioning, the players would have more energy at the end of the season. If we recruited better players. If we practiced more. If I had new assistants. I always focused on the obvious tangible things—lack of talent, poor support staff, bad facilities, bad weather.

"It's very easy for a coach to fall into this trap. It's much easier to blame tangible, external things than it is to look inward and find out what intangible things might be holding us back from our true potential. It is hard to look at ourselves. The last thing we want to admit to ourselves, let alone to others, is that we are the problem, that we only have ourselves to blame.

"The 1996 season was bad in every way possible. We had good players, but we barely stayed above .500 and missed the league tournament. There were problems with team chemistry, people problems, tension among the staff—all of which had been there before but had been camouflaged by winning.

"It was during that year that my two assistant coaches aggressively began to complain about each other to me and, I later learned, to others about me. There is a fine line between being a delegator and a dictator. I was trying to give the assistants more responsibility because they had been with me for several years. Instead of delegating authority in certain areas while maintaining overall control, however, I was essentially abdicating my role as head coach to my assistants. Each assistant had, by default, his own team, and I had none."

RICK:

"No staff development was going on here. John was simply giving his assistants the keys and then leaving them alone. A good leader develops other good leaders. John's job was to develop his assistant coaches. But when John allowed his assistants to function autonomously—when he stopped developing his staff and acting as a potent leader—he ended up with separate teams and a host of problems.

"When John lost control of his assistants, he also lost their respect. They went off to do their own thing because that is how they protected themselves. When we don't get strong leadership, we tend to build protective walls around ourselves, which insulate and protect us, but also isolate us from others. It's a common coping strategy.

"The same problems were recurring each year, only they were getting worse with time. More and more symptoms were appearing. It was like an illness spreading through the body, worsening until finally John had to admit, 'I have to go see a doctor. I need some help.'

"John and his staff had begun to look individually at finding solutions to the problems that were plaguing the team. Now, after a very disappointing season, the hurt was bad enough for the staff to come together and to seek solutions as a group.

"Everyone felt an internal readiness for change. If that feeling isn't there, nothing really changes. By the end of the horror show that was the 1996 season, the feeling was definitely there. The team was ready for some tough self-examination."

Before we talk too much about the process of change, we want to make clear that it isn't necessary to bring in a professional psychologist like Rick to help manage change. Almost anyone who has had some experience working with groups, is familiar with the program, and is acceptable to the people involved could act as a facilitator. This person might be another coach, an educator, an administrator, or a member of the clergy. The job of the facilitator is to help initiate a process for change, not produce a detailed blueprint of exactly how that change will take place. One advantage of using a professional therapist, though, is that he or she has had both the training and the experience to remain focused on the objectives and not let personal feelings, biases, or agendas get in the way.

If you don't have access to the services of a professional, you need to be aware that this is a process that can cause considerable stress. The prospect of change can create eager anticipation—"at last, we're going to do something"—but it also can create a lot of pain. Self-examination is difficult. Accepting responsibility, however, is an essential part of overcoming The Other Stuff. We see it as a sign of health.

RICK:
"No one should ever coach alone. I don't care what level you're at, you should always have someone you trust available to you. This person could be a paid assistant, a volunteer, or just someone you go to for advice once in a while. When you're alone, you're much more vulnerable. You can become enmeshed  in the system in such a way that you lose perspective on anything outside the system. But if you have someone advising you who can stand with one foot in and one foot out of the program, you're much more likely to gain new perspectives on both yourself and your program."

As the summer of 1996 began, John felt that he was coaching alone. So did each of his assistants. Each was frustrated and suspicious of the other. But each was also ready to commit to the process of change. The hard part was getting them all to sit down and share their gripes, laments, and points of view.

JOHN:
"Everyone had their own opinions about what was or was not working in the program, but we weren't sharing our ideas with each other. The assistants were sharing their concerns with friends, other coaches, and scouts—people they trusted. Some of  this information was coming back to me indirectly, but only in bits and pieces: Neither assistant would speak directly to the other, and I was almost completely out of the loop.

"Because I was not providing sufficient leadership, the pitching coach was off on his own with his pitchers, essentially running his own practice with his own team. The position coach was off with his players doing this own thing. Each doubted the other's ability, and each felt he had to take care of his "team" exclusively. Meanwhile, I was alone in the middle with no one to coach. All I'm hearing from either of them is that the other is an idiot and I'm doing a terrible job. Each was doing his best to separate himself from what he perceived to be his main problems: the other assistant and the head coach.

"The wheels had come off, and it's not too hard to figure out why—now. At the time, though, we hadn't yet identified the real problem. It wasn't the competition, it wasn't the talent, it wasn't the university's location, it wasn't the facilities. These are small things. We were the problem. The situation was so bad, we were all looking for other jobs. Still, we rationalized that if only this guy would leave or that guy would be fired, all our problems would be over. We still didn't get it."

RICK:

"The situation with John's program was not much different than that of a family whose relationships have become increasingly damaged or have started to break down. In such a case, everybody gets so wrapped up in their own individual worlds that they neglect dealing with each other as a family. Without knowing quite why or how, individual family members are moving off in directions that don't feel right to the group as a whole. The family isn't working effectively as a unit."

When You're at the Bottom....

Even though the pain was becoming more and more obvious, Rick restrained himself from intervening in the program. He knew that the worst thing he could do would be to push his way into the center of things and tell people, "Okay, this is how it is has to be!" He also knew from his experience as a therapist that things had to get really bad before they could get better.

COACHING COACHES

At the end of the '96 season, things had gotten really bad. Everything seemed to be falling apart in John's life—his family, his program, his career. He was hurting enough to be ready for real change—hurting enough that he asked Rick to sit in on some staff meetings.

JOHN:
"During those first critical meetings together, Rick helped us define our working environment. Each staff member took turns lambasting the system. One assistant complained that the administration didn't seem to care about the baseball program. He was right; they don't, at least not to the degree they care about some of the other sports programs. Another assistant complained that, because of a revision of Big Ten policy, we had lost two scholarships. He was also right, but there was no use in getting upset about it. Some things are out of our control. We're not bad coaches just because we can't control everything. We have to accept this fact and not let it affect our performance.

"Each of us in those meetings thought he knew the reasons why the team was struggling, and those reasons usually involved blaming other coaches and complaining about problems that were out of our control. The truth lay elsewhere, and we had to face it, however unpleasant it was."

RICK:

"It's easy to blame everything and everyone but yourself when bad things start happening. There are a lot of reasons why things go wrong, but making excuses doesn't fix them. You need to step back and take a look at yourself and figure out how you may be contributing to the problem.

"In John's case there were serious differences between perception and reality. His perception was that the Gopher baseball team was special, even unique. This perception was a fantasy. The reality was that there were programs out there every bit as good as the Minnesota Gopher program, and some of these were succeeding where the University of Minnesota program was not.

"It's up to the leader to define reality for his staff and players. If he or she doesn't have a realistic definition, the rest of people in the program won't either."

From the beginning of Rick's involvement with the program, he had been meeting with and talking to the players. But Rick couldn't, for reasons of confidentiality, tell John exactly what was going on in these kids' heads in relation to problems the team was experiencing. Also, Rick thought it would be better if the staff dealt with their problems without worrying about what the players thought.

JOHN:

"Rick helped the staff begin to communicate more directly. He was not the instrument of change per se, but he kept the process focused and productive. I'm sure the information he got from the players helped him help us. He was able to use that information in subtle ways without breaking confidences.

"During the meetings with the staff, Rick would guide the discussions, giving us bits and pieces of information that would ultimately help us figure things out on our own. He wasn't doing it for us. He never said, 'This is how it has to be.' That wasn't his function. If he had forced us to do something, it wouldn't have worked in the long run. He got us to think about our problems without shoving solutions down our throats.

"I see now that he was coaching us by offering a model for dealing with problems. This model is the way we now like to coach our players. We give them information and try to help them figure things out, but we don't do it for them. We've became better coaches by not trying to do everything for our players."

REALISTIC EXPECTATIONS

JOHN:

"One of the more important things we learned in our meetings was that we had been setting unrealistic expectations for our players and ourselves. I remember one meeting where everybody spilled their guts out about what they didn't like—what they thought we were doing wrong, where they thought the problems were, who they thought was responsible.

Some of the things we complained about we realized we couldn't change. We couldn't change the weather. We couldn't change the location of the school. We couldn't change the fact that our scholarships had been reduced to nine. We had to accept these facts and deal with them.

"We also realized that we were always asking the players to try harder when they were already putting out their best efforts. All we were doing by pressuring them was to make it more difficult for them to perform well. 'If we just try harder, if we take a hundred more swings, if we run a little bit more, we'll win more.' Lack of effort wasn't the problem. I don't think it was ever the problem."

RICK:

"The staff had been mistaking effort for effectiveness. It's possible, for example, for players to give their best effort in practice without that translating into effective play on the field. Sometimes we make kids do the same things over and over again without really analyzing if there's a payoff. And often it is the highest achieving or most competitive kid who's going to keep trying and trying as hard as he can until he starts to smoke and burn out. Here's what you have to ask yourself: Why keep doing something the same way, over and over, when it's clear it's not working? Why push kids to do more of something that's already proved ineffective? Why not try something different?"

Teamwork is More than a Cliché

After some intense sessions during the off-season of 1996, the coaches were finally talking together. They pledged to communicate directly and to exercise stronger leadership. No one believed the process was complete, but they had made a good start.

One of the first things John did was write a mission statement for the program. The statement not only helped him to put things in perspective but also gave his coaches and players clear goals for change. John presented the mission statement at a staff retreat before the start of fall practice. The other coaches discussed it, made some minor revisions, and then signed off on it. Most, however, were still a little wary. Would the positive changes they could see in John withstand the pressure of the season? Would the assistants really be able to continue to communicate with each other? And perhaps the biggest question: How would the players react to the process of change?

John introduced the players to the mission statement at the beginning of fall practice of 1996. The statement clearly laid out his vision and expectations for the program. It was the cornerstone on which John would rebuild the team. By drafting, defending, and publishing the mission statement, John was saying, "This is who I am. This is where I want to go." He was defining his "I" position.

Overcoming "Tradition"

JOHN:

"We had a number of seniors on the 1996–1997 team, and most of them were resistant to change. They just wanted to play out their final season the "traditional" way. Throughout fall practice, the staff worked on a program to get the kids to take ownership of the team and of their own actions, but most of the seniors didn't want to take ownership of anything.

"A key item in the mission statement was eliminating hazing and the privileges of seniority. Kids grew up believing that hazing was bonding. We saw it as creating division and animosity. When they were in ninth grade, the older kids dumped on them. They, in turn, couldn't wait to dump on the next class. The seniors on our team had typically treated the freshmen like dirt. Now we were telling the team that everyone would be equal in terms of responsibility and privilege. The coaches would say, 'Here's what has to be done, you guys figure out who does what.' Each player was responsible for carrying his own equipment and for helping keep the locker room clean; these were not duties to be delegated entirely to underclassmen.

"Many of the seniors were angry. They didn't want to lose the privileges they thought they had earned. They were not buying what we were selling.

"Changing long-standing practices or traditions is difficult and takes time. That was driven home to me when I got a call from the athletic director one night in late fall informing me there was some serious drinking and partying going on in one of the dorms and baseball players were involved. He told me to drive in to campus, stop what was going on, and report back to him.

"I found a bunch of really drunk freshman, including two who had passed out. The dorm manager had called for the paramedics and had informed campus police. What was happening, of course, was a rite of initiation—something that had been going on for years. I made sure that the sick players got proper care and that the rest went back to their rooms. The media got hold of the story, and the athletic director had to discipline the players under the provisions of the university drug and alcohol policy. The whole thing was a mess. It was the last time the seniors got to have their way."

A battle for structure was again being staged. This skirmish went to the senior players and the old ways of doing things. For John it was a painful slap in the face. He knew that he still had much to do in order to reclaim his program. Just writing a mission statement wasn't going to do it.

After warning the team that such conduct would no longer be tolerated, John used the incident as a teaching opportunity. The players learned why the staff was trying to stop this type of hazing by upperclassmen. The point was that such traditions didn't bring the team together. It created divisions within the team.

With the athletic director's permission, John wrote to the parents of each member of the team, explaining what had happened and telling them that, in John's opinion, each player bore responsibility for the incident. Everyone's academic record would now list a first offense against the university drug and alcohol policy. Everyone would be penalized. John also told the parents that he was to blame as well in that the incident resulted from a tradition that had developed in a program for which he was responsible.

JOHN:
"At the next team meeting I told the players that the only way this tradition was going stop was if the current freshmen stopped it. If they continued the same destructive hazing practices with the next class, it would never stop. I said to them, 'If this happens again next year, I'm going to hold you people personally accountable. You will be asked to leave the program.'

"Did that mean players wouldn't drink alcohol anymore? I wasn't that naïve. But, under my watch, there were going to be no more initiations involving alcohol."

New Beginnings

Even with the hazing incident, John and the staff sensed that things were improving. They had made progress in their sessions with Rick and now were looking for an effective method of positive reinforcement to use with the players. They needed something concrete and visible to represent the changes in the program to the players.

THE "M" CAP

The staff agreed to try a variation on a program John had heard about from Augie Garrido, a fellow coach on the USA team and the head baseball coach at the University of Texas. Garrido had replaced a legend on the Austin campus and taken over a program wracked by scandal. As part of his battle for structure—imposing his stamp on a program in need of change—the new coach took away the players' caps with the "T" and gave them plain orange caps. In order for a player to get his "T" back, he had to earn it, and earn it according to criteria set down by the new coach and his staff.

JOHN:
"We began our version of the cap program with the start of winter practice, soon after the alcohol incident. The staff decided to issue plain maroon caps to all but five players. The coaches selected the five not for their athletic prowess or class rank but for their attitude, classroom attendance, and sense of responsibility to themselves and others. One was a nonstarter, and only one was a senior.

"We wanted the other players to think about why we had singled out those five players and to discuss the issue among themselves: 'Why does that guy have an "M" and I don't? What do I need to do to get one?'

"We told all the players our expectations of them when we discussed the mission statement at the beginning of fall practice. However, we never told anyone what the exact criteria were to earn the "M." We did announce that if you didn't earn your "M," you weren't going to play in any games. That got everyone's attention in a hurry. We also told them that getting the "M" didn't mean you couldn't lose it if you screwed up, and that it would be a lot harder to get it back than to acquire it the first time. That caused them to think, too.

"Many of the players thought that showing up for practice and trying hard was enough. They became frustrated when just doing the same thing over and over didn't earn them the magic cap. We would tell them that showing up and trying were minimum requirements, not reasons to get the "M." They also had to have a positive attitude, show up for class, and conduct themselves in a responsible manner. We were trying to develop a sense of ownership on the part of the players.

"The coaches have only limited contact with the players. We don't go to class with them and aren't with them in the dorms or fraternity houses. As more and more players figured out what was required of them and received their "M" cap, they put the pressure on the kids who weren't going to class or were not making the effort in other ways. It became the players' program, not the coaches'.

"In fact, one time the staff was involved in a meeting that ran late, and we missed the first part of a team meeting. The players wanted to take away our "M." We thought about it but decided against it. Not only did we have a legitimate reason to be late, but, more important, it reminded them that we are not players. We are coaches. We are different.

"The program is designed to teach responsibility and ownership, but it is not intended to put players in charge."

> ## Rick:
>
> "The generational boundary we drew between parent and child in Section 2 can be applied to the relationship between coach and player, too. Coaches are the parents, and players are the children. Just as with parents, there sometimes are things coaches need to do that have nothing to do with the players and are really none of their business. If John had allowed the players to punish the coaches for missing part of a meeting, this boundary would have been blurred. That, in turn, would have made it very difficult to continue the process of change. It was important for the coaches to make clear to the players that they occupied a different position within the program than the players did."

One Step at a Time

The "M" cap program had its problems that first year. When a very good player was in danger of losing his "M" and being benched, John left the decision on the player's status to the team. The team voted to let the infractions go. The senior-dominated squad could only change so much. The win-loss record didn't change much, either. The 1997 team again missed the Big Ten tournament and finished with a record comparable to the year before.

But John had begun the process. One technique that was successful with the players was the "quote of the day." Each day at the beginning of practice, a designated player had to read a favorite quotation and tell what it meant to him. The activity increased communication between the players and provided insights into the players that their teammates and coaches might not otherwise have had. John was beginning to understand what it would take to reestablish himself as the head coach in deed as well as name. He also could now reflect honestly on his own problems and the role they had played in the breakdown of the program.

Needed: A Head Coach in Charge

Before John could fully reinstitute his leadership of the University of Minnesota baseball program, he first had to come to terms with who he was as a person and a coach.

JOHN:

"During the 1997 season, I began to realize that I had lost track of who I was as a person and what I wanted to be. Rick described me later as a sailboat without a centerboard. I was wandering all over the place. My aimlessness had a negative effect on my relationship with my family. When things weren't going well, blaming others, including my spouse, became easy. But she wasn't the problem; the problem was me.

"I went to Rick for help because my world was falling apart—that's how bad the hurt was. Rick told me bluntly: 'John, you're the problem. You have to decide who you are and what kind of person you want to be. Don't look at all these other people and situations; take a look at yourself. Only when you redefine who you are as a person will you be able to redefine yourself as a husband, father, and coach.'

"Looking at myself honestly was very painful. I'd always had a caretaker personality. It was the role I'd played in my family growing up, and it was the role I was still trying to play in all my other relationships. I wouldn't do things to make me happy; I was always trying to make everybody else happy, and, consequently, I wasn't getting what I wanted out of my career or personal life. I didn't like to be criticized, and when that happened, I became even more of a caretaker. I wanted to make everyone happy so they wouldn't criticize me.

"I had to learn to quit being so accommodating. I had to learn to stand up and say, 'This is what I want.' I had to do that even if it meant hurting someone else or possibly losing a relationship, because if I'm not happy, how can I make anyone else happy? If I don't know who I am, how can I define roles for others in my interactions or relationships with them?"

RICK:

"Under stress, we tend to revert to behaviors that we're comfortable with. These behaviors aren't necessarily healthy, just comfortable. When John was under stress, his caretaker personality took over. John was trying so hard to make things better for everyone else that he failed to take care of himself."

TIME TO LAY IT ON THE LINE

A conversation with a friend and fellow coach helped John advance the process of building more honest and open communications among his coaching staff. The coach had brought his team to Minneapolis to play in the Hormel Classic in March of 1997. During the three-day period of the tournament, the coach had observed the dissension on John's coaching staff. He also had heard comments from other coaches during the course of the season, such as 'Those guys don't get along,' 'The staff doesn't like each other,' 'Each of them is doing his own thing,' and so on. His observations confirmed what he had been hearing.

John and the other coach sat together during the College World Series at the end of the 1997 season. The coach told John as a friend that the word was out that John's assistants were disloyal. He also suggested that, while he didn't know what all the problems were, John didn't have to put up with open criticism from his staff.

John thanked him but told him that, in fact, the main problem wasn't the assistants, but John himself.

JOHN:
"I told the staff what the coach had said. Afterwards, I told them that I expected them to get on the same page with me and work together to resolve our differences. I also told them that I was going to take firm ownership of the program and give them clearer direction in the future. I let them know that it was my program. If they wanted to come together and work with me, that was great. If they didn't, I would find someone else who would.

"I told them, 'You guys are all looking for other jobs. I've been looking, too. You know what? None of us is going to find another job if we don't get our act together. If you think you're going to get a new job based on your performance here, you're kidding yourself.'"

RICK:
"One of the key qualities of a good leader is the ability to define reality for his or her group. But for some time, John had had reality defined for him by others. What John's staff and his players needed was someone who could tell it straight. John needed to come to them and say, 'Look guys, we're not getting it done. This isn't good enough.' Sometimes defining reality means delivering hard messages, and that's what John had to do."

John was making considerable progress in regaining control of himself and his program. If there was one thing that illustrated that progress, it was the replacement of a volunteer coach.

FOR THE GOOD OF THE PROGRAM

Sometimes coaches must make a change that affects someone who has been a part of the program for a long time. John faced such a situation at the end of the 1997 season. A volunteer coach had been at every game and practice during John's entire career as head coach. He had been a mentor to John and a friend.

JOHN:

"As part of the evaluation of the program, I had to examine the volunteer coach position honestly and do what was best for the program. I concluded that what we were not getting what we needed out of the position. I had to make a change.

"It was difficult decision, but I knew I had to put my personal feelings aside and do what was in the best interest of the program. The work I had done with Rick, and the more open and honest communication I was now enjoying with the assistants, helped me make a tough decision."

RICK:

"John's decision to replace the volunteer coach sent a message to both staff and players that John was serious about following through on things he deemed necessary to enable change and growth. The assistant coaches had been looking to John to see if the change was real. Replacing the volunteer coach showed them that their boss was ready to make the tough decisions in order to move ahead. The players also learned that their head coach and his united staff were committed to doing whatever was best for the program."

Putting it Together

By the end of the summer of 1997, the various elements of John's program were coming together in at least a loose formation. John had emerged from a period of self-examination and understanding to take charge of the staff and the program once again. Those freshman who had been abused by the upperclassmen were now sophomores and had no desire to go back to the way things had been. There was a new crop of freshman who neither knew nor cared about the past.

One of the first events of the new academic year was a two-day team outing at which new and returning players met and began to bond. Also that fall, John established mandatory team meetings on Sunday nights. It was a difficult decision, but John wanted to be sure that the players were aware of their responsibilities to themselves and to their teammates.

JOHN:

"There was a considerable controversy when we started the team meetings—6:00 p.m. every Sunday night. Many of the players were annoyed at having to give up their time and thought the whole concept was BS. Some of them still feel this way.

"The proof is in the pudding. We will never be able to accumulate the talent that a Stanford and Florida State can, so we have to do find other ways to compete. Improving team chemistry and empowering the players to think for themselves are two competitive strategies we can put in place. At the team meetings, the guys learn to question, to think, to communicate. We're building a core group that really believes in our program."

RICK:

"One of the things the coaches and I tried to do was to have the players expand their thinking. For example, we discussed effort vs. effectiveness, and tried to get the players to understand that you can put out all the effort in the world, but if you don't achieve effective results, you're just wasting your time. To be effective you have to expand your boundaries. That was and continues to be true for John and his assistants, but it also applies to the players. It's easy to stay within a comfort zone, and hard to step outside it and try something different.

"To illustrate the point, I like to use an exercise involving the following diagram.

"The exercise is to connect all nine dots using four straight lines without lifting your pencil from the paper or retracing a line. Many of you might be familiar with this, but if you're not, try it.

"I once gave the exercise to a player who kept getting stuck trying to solve his problem in a conventional way. The dots demonstrated looking at a problem in a new way.

"The player spent a whole hour and never solved the problem. He came in the next week and worked on it again without success, but wouldn't let me give him the answer. Finally, a couple of weeks later, he came in with a big grin on his face.

"'You solved the puzzle, didn't you?' I asked.

"He nodded. 'You wouldn't believe how. I was cursing you up and down, working on it night and day. I had papers all over, and I was just driving my girlfriend nuts. Finally I just said "screw this" and threw it away. Then this morning I'm driving to the ballpark and I'm listening to the radio and I stop at a stop sign and I hear this song and for some reason, out of the blue, it hits me, the answer.' Sure enough, he'd figured it out—he had expanded his boundaries."

TRUST THE PROCESS

One of the reasons the teams made major strides in the 1997-98 season was that there was now a core of players who'd been through the first year of the new program and believed strongly that the process was working. The returning players knew who they were as individuals and as a team, and they all agreed that they were not going to tolerate another 30–26 season.

The incoming freshmen were made to feel a part of the team; there was no hazing or humiliation of underclassmen. Passive at first, the freshman gradually began to participate in the team meetings, drawn out by activities planned by the coaching staff.

All the coaches were responsible for planning and moderating the team meetings—even the new, young volunteer coach. From the coaches, the players received the consistent message that the staff was united under the leadership of the head coach.

This was a team of equals. For the first time under John's tenure, there were no captains. Everyone was expected to contribute equally and to do his fair share of the work. The emphasis was on being accountable for your actions, supporting your teammates, and committing to the goals of the program. These goals included managing emotions, setting realistic expectations, and playing relaxed, one out at a time.

JOHN:

"It's easy to sell a program during fall practice. It's much harder to stay the course during the season when things can and do get screwed up.

"We were tested the first game of the season against Nebraska. They tied us in the top of the ninth on a defensive mistake. I wondered how the kids were going to respond. Were they going to panic? Get angry at the guy who made the error? Lose their cool—and the game in the process? But they didn't panic or get angry or lose their cool. They stayed relaxed and kept their heads in the game, which we won in extra innings. It was a defining moment for this young team. They found a way to win instead of an excuse for losing. A lot of the guys then began to understand what we had been talking about.

"Because of the inhospitable climate in Minnesota, we usually scheduled a number of early season games in warm-weather states. This year we had scheduled several games in California, included a tournament in San Diego. We were to open the tournament against the University of Washington, which was then a top-twenty team. The day of the game, it was pouring rain, and we had to get on a bus and drive three hours to Yuma, Arizona, to get the game in. In the old days, this would have given the kids an excuse for playing poorly. Not now. The kids got off the bus, took the field, and proceeded to hammer the Huskies. The team was focused; they weren't thinking about anything but the game. I was proud of them and told them so."

The coaches continually reinforced John's message. After winning seven of the eight games in California, some of the kids began to talk prematurely about playing in the NCAA tournament. The staff refocused the kids on winning one game at a time.

Just before the start of the Big Ten season, the Minnesota Gophers lost their best pitcher to injury. The team promptly lost its first two games, and five games in two weekends. Here was another great opportunity to teach. With encouragement from the coaches, the players settled down and began to play much better, finishing a close second to Illinois in the regular conference season. The Gophers then swept the conference postseason tournament at Illinois to garner an automatic NCAA bid. John and his staff were pleased both with the performance of the players and their attitude. Going into the NCAA tourney, the Gophers stood 45-13. Some people were even starting to fantasize about the College World Series.

JOHN:

"The NCAA regional was at Stanford, which has one of the better baseball programs in the country. I think our kids were a bit in awe of the whole experience. The first game was against Alabama, a top-ten ranked team. We were leading in the seventh when we suddenly forgot the lessons we'd learned during the season, and started counting outs. We had been able to deal with the pressure of the Big Ten tournament, but, here, the pressure got to us. We ended up losing in the ninth inning and then got hammered by Stanford in the next game. Our season ended 45 –15, a successful season both in terms of our win-loss record wins and the progress we'd made as a team.

"Although the team slid back into some old habits in the NCAA tournament, they accepted their losses as constructive learning experiences that would help them handle future high-pressure situations more effectively. Despite my disappointment at losing, I was encouraged by the knowledge that the team had moved beyond its old ways of thinking and acting. We had a good nucleus of kids coming back, kids who were solidly behind the new way we were doing things."

Accept Change and Move Ahead

The baseball program at the University of Minnesota had improved greatly under John's guidance during the 1997-98 year. The team's winning record clearly reflected this improvement. Now came another test of John's program: the resignation of a key assistant.

The pitching coach, who had been with John for eleven years, was offered a Division I head coaching job. Because communication had improved between John and his staff, John had known of the impending offer for some time. The two men had been talking about it since the other university had sent out its first feelers.

JOHN:

"I genuinely can't tell how I would have reacted to the situation a couple of years earlier. Even after all the changes Rick had helped me make, I have to confess that replacing a coach was a hassle. But I was better prepared to deal with it because of the changes I had made in the program over the previous several years.

"I was as excited about the 1998–1999 season as I've ever been about any season in my coaching career. Not just because the team stayed remarkably intact—we lost fewer players to the pros than I expected—but because I knew I was going to be working with a new pitching coach. Rick once told the team that the Chinese denote crisis with two words: 'danger' and 'opportunity.' I had confidence that the program was well positioned to deal with both the inevitable problems that would crop up and with the opportunities that would present themselves."

The 1998–1999 season marked the first time that a majority of players on the team had at least one year's experience with the new program, so, although he began the season without a pitching coach, John was not distracted from his head coaching duties. With his new program solidly in place, John was able to rely on the more experienced players to help train their newer teammates. The veterans willingly jumped in and took the lead.

JOHN:

"I went to the veteran pitchers and told them, 'You know what the routine is for stretches and throwing. Either I can stand here telling you everything to do, or you can do it on your own and teach the new players how we do it here.'

"Not only did the pitchers manage their own prep time, but they also drew up their own practice plans. It's great. I'm in charge. The kids know that. But they've taken responsibility for themselves whenever I've asked them. In fact, I was working with one of our new pitchers on a particular move when one of the other guys came over and said, 'Coach, I think I can help. I know the move and can teach the new guy what he needs to know. You have a bunch of other things to do.'

"Now that player may not teach the move exactly the way I would, and I would still want to monitor to see if the freshman is doing it right—but that's not the point. There's no way, even a year before, that a player would have had the awareness and maturity to even think of helping out in that situation. It's remarkable to say the least, and a credit to the kids in the program."

Rick:

"I noticed two good changes right from the start of practice. First, the kids weren't standing around waiting for the coaches to tell them what to do. They were exhibiting much more of a sense of ownership of the team. They noticed what was going on around them and monitored appropriate behavior in themselves and in others.

"Second, the guys were much more willing to talk to one another. If someone wasn't living up to a commitment he'd made, another player would take him aside and remind him of it. It was the same for team meetings. Rather than introduce himself, each player would introduce the player next to him. One kid who had been very shy and quiet during the previous year was introduced by his teammate as "our speech communications major." Everyone had a good laugh, including the player, who had matured significantly in his ability to participate, communicate, and contribute over the last year. He knew from experience that both he and his opinions would be treated with respect by his coaches and his peers."

From Understanding to Ownership

The primary goal that Rick and John set for 1998–1999 was to transform the players' understanding of the theory of ownership into actual practice. The constructive way the players had reacted to the absence of a pitching coach indicated that that they were already beginning to do this.

This goal was complicated when John's volunteer coach accepted an assistant position at another university and John suddenly found himself having to fill two coaching positions—half his staff.

JOHN:

"In previous years, when interviewing assistants, I had looked primarily for skills, experience, and the willingness to put up with all the tedious duties assistants must perform. Now I was looking primarily for people with open minds, people who could fit into the new culture we'd created, a culture  very different from that of most other programs. Skill and experience were still important, but credentials alone wouldn't make the assistant a good coach.

"I was fortunate to find exactly what I was looking for. The new volunteer coach had experience in Division II and III programs and was ready to move into a new type of environment at a higher level. The new pitching coach had been a minor league pitching coach for twelve years. He, too, was ready for a change and a new challenge, and was receptive to the culture of our program."

As open as the new pitching coach was to working within the culture of John's program, he was a bit nervous at first. So were the players. They feared that the culture they had just adapted to might change again.

RICK:

"Change is stressful. The changes over the previous few years have been stressful for the players, and now, just when things seemed to be stabilizing, here came the threat of more change.

"The players were concerned that they were going to get a pitching coach who would tell them what to do and how to do it—a 'my way or the highway' approach. But one of the first things the new coach did was to allow the players

---

to call their own pitches. This allayed the players' fears, for now they had more responsibility, not less, and they knew they were being challenged.

"At the end-of-year banquet, the new coach spoke about the importance of taking ownership—how at first he had felt that he was the new guy, that the program wasn't his, but how he had made it his over time."

Several incidents during the year pointed to the fact that the players were taking appropriate ownership of their roles within the program.

- Everyone received a golden "M" on their cap at the beginning of the season, and it was up to the players to decide which team members, if any, were worthy of wearing it. During a team meeting without coaches, each player was challenged by the rest of the team to defend his right to wear the "M." Several players, including some of the team leaders, acknowledged that they had not been meeting the minimum requirements and voluntarily turned in their "M." Some first-year players also asked for plain caps, saying they didn't yet fully understand the requirements and preferred to earn their "M."

- An assistant coach began to revert to the team's old habit of letting emotions rule actions. After a particularly ugly win, he lost control and yelled about the lousy field, the lousy umpires, and the lousy players. John didn't have to take the coach aside, though, because one of the players got there first and told the coach that he needed to exercise more self-control. The next day, a sign appeared on the dugout wall that read "C.Y.F.E." "I made the sign as a reminder," the coach explained. "The 'C' stands for 'Control,' the 'Y' for 'Your,' the 'F' for 'Feelings,' and the 'E' for 'Emotions.'" The sign accompanied the team from game to game the rest of the year.

- A freshman who wasn't practicing hard was confronted by one of the team leaders (again without any intervention by John) and warned that his effort was not acceptable, that the team was counting on him and he was going to have to play harder. Because the message was delivered by one of the team's stars—a sure major league draft choice—the freshman took it to heart and went on to have a fine season.

RICK:

"These incidents illustrated a real shift. Instead of the coaches always telling the players what to do and how to do it, the kids were teaching and motivating themselves. The will to succeed was coming from inside the players rather than outside.

"Many coaches who run their programs with a traditional, top-down approach complain that their kids don't care or try hard enough. The problem is often that the players feel no ownership in the program.

"What we saw in the 1998–1999 season was desire and ownership coming from within the team. The players took care of each other, supported each other, and policed each other. The team's performance on the field bore out the effectiveness of the approach. The team wasn't the most talented in the country, but it played well enough to win a school record forty-six games and come just short of a trip to the College World Series."

John:

"At the beginning of the season, our top four pitchers were injured. Rather than using this adversity as an excuse, the team took it as an opportunity for growth. Pitchers who would play key roles later in the season got valuable game experience. Not one of the team's first fifteen wins went to a pitcher we'd identified as a top starter before the season began.

"During this year, my father became gravely ill, and he died just after the season ended. The team expressed concern for me and my family, but I'm convinced they took charge of the program no more or no less than if I'd had no family concerns."

An Unfinished Story

Change and renewal are now the ongoing tradition in the Minnesota baseball program. Rick and John will always have to reinforce the fundamentals of responsibility and communication, just as the coaches have to drill the fundamentals of the game. But, now, the core of the team has a new tradition—not a static 'this is the way we've always done things' tradition, but a tradition of continuous self-examination and adaptation.

JOHN:

"Most of us will say that our job as a coach is to help kids learn something constructive from their mistakes and failures. Bad times provide opportunities to teach and learn.

"What's true for kids is also true for coaches. If we're going to survive and thrive in this business, we have to figure out how to do for ourselves what we try to do for the kids we coach: turn difficult and stressful times into constructive learning opportunities.

"I've gone through some pretty rugged times, but what I've learned about myself in the process will benefit me, my family, my program, and my career for a long time to come. It's a continuing process. I'll know more about myself in a year than I know now. I'll know more about my family, too. And my assistants and players. Only when this process of self-examination and change stops will the old problems start creeping back in."

Section Five

It All Comes Back to You (With a Little Help)

The Other Stuff Isn't Going to Go Away

Throughout this book, we have shared with you our thoughts and feelings about coaching in the hope that what we've learned, sometimes painfully, in our careers will help you become a more successful and happier coach. We began by considering the inner coach—how a coach defines himself or herself. We then looked at the coach's relationships with those persons most affected by his or her job. Continuing to move outward, we pointed out some of the landmines a coach can step on that can severely cripple or even end a coaching career, and we described some of the dozens of duties a coach must perform in addition to working with players on skill development and game strategies. And, finally, we provided a practical illustration of our ideas using John Anderson's baseball program at the University of Minnesota as a real-world example.

Although we are most experienced with professional and university programs, we have pointedly tried to include examples from community, youth, and K–12 sports programs whenever possible. We continue to be deeply concerned over the state of youth and community-based athletic programs. They are the starting point for many of the negative aspects of organized sports that contribute to burn-out in both athletes and coaches. We'd like to sum up now our ideas about how best to prevent such burn-out, and how to survive and thrive in the world of modern sports.

PLAYING (AND COACHING) OUT OF DESPERATION VS. PLAYING (AND COACHING) OUT OF DESIRE

Why are so many coaches afraid to encourage kids to play out of desire alone, to compete just for the fun of it? Perhaps they worry that if their players are internally motivated they won't be able to control them. Or that if the players think and act independently they won't stay committed to the program.

We disagree. We believe that coaching is about using sports to help kids grow as individuals. Athletes will perform better over the long haul if they're actively choosing to play. Kids should play because they want to, not because they feel they have to. Many coaches don't agree. They argue, "It's okay for a person to want to play, but I want a person who is desperate to play—one who needs to be here and will do whatever it takes to win."

We think there are holes in that reasoning. When kids plays out of desperation rather than desire, their identity may come to rest entirely on who they are as a player. When the pressures of the game build up, the kids burn out prematurely.

It's possible to exploit a player's desperation and dependency and get great results: a great home run hitter, a great quarterback, a great goalie. The player may eventually burn out, but for a while, at least, he or she shines. We rationalize such burnout by thinking "At least we got a building built," or "At least we won a championship while the kid was here." We're sorry about the kid's problems, but, hey, they're not our problems—we're on to our next group of players.

What passes for athletic commitment with some coaches—say, a player attending practice instead of the birth of his child—is something really more akin to fear. Athletes who perform because they have to are ultimately going to be unhappy at what they're doing and will create problems for their coach. They may perform well for a time, but they will not be able to maintain their performance over a long period.

RICK:

"In order to reach his or her full potential as an athlete, a young person must feel free to quit. Only when you can choose to quit can you really choose to play. When I ask someone if he or she has the freedom to quit and the answer is 'no,' then I know that player is trapped and cannot perform up to his or her full potential.

"A fear of failure is being instilled in our young athletes. Kids are burning out in high school and college because they just can't handle the pressure. The game isn't a game to them anymore. It isn't fun. They're working, not playing. But they can't quit because they are so terribly afraid of hurting their parents, disappointing their peers, letting their coaches down. People have lived vicariously through them for years, dreaming of varsity letters, major college scholarships, and million-dollar contracts. Although the kids have a much better chance of being hit by lightning than becoming professional athletes, the expectations build anyway.

"These athletes think, 'I've invested my whole life in this sport. I've got to continue.' Then they end up defining themselves as good or bad depending on the outcome of a single game. This is a terrible burden to place on an adult, let alone a youngster.

"Coaches who try to lift this burden off their young players often find that they have to carry a heavy burden themselves. The pressures put on athletes by parents, fans, and administrators can weigh just as heavily on coaches. Like athletes, coaches must feel free to quit if they are going to be truly effective at their jobs. Coaches who are internally motivated and independent do a better job of teaching their players to be internally motivated and independent. Such coaches tend to make decisions based on the long-term welfare of their players rather than on short-term pay-offs. When coaches have the freedom to say 'I can quit,' both they and their players are more likely to perform up to their full potential."

SUSTAINED OPTIMAL PERFORMANCE

When coaches encourage their players to dissociate their sense of self from their performance on the field, they run a certain risk. Parents, staff, administrators, even the players themselves may complain that they are not being "tough and demanding enough." Similarly, coaches run a risk when they try to dissociate their own sense of self from the job of coaching. Others may perceive this as a lack of commitment or seriousness on the part of the coach. But an enlightened few—not many yet, but the number's growing—are beginning to understand that defining yourself by external measures is a sure path to loneliness and dissatisfaction. "I worked all my life to get to this point and to make all this money, yet I feel an emptiness inside," says one coach. Another wonders why all her relationships—even with her family—seem to be falling apart. A third realizes that by defining himself externally for so many years, he has lost his identity, his sense of who he really is.

Rick:

"Two points: One, coaches are like athletes in that they tend to define who they are based on what they do on the field. If you win, you're a good person. If not....Over the long run, the ups and downs are going to drive you nuts.

"Number two, most coaches are nervous around an athlete who is internally motivated and independent. They prefer that their players sacrifice themselves to point of misery, that they become totally dependent on the coach and the team. 'If you want to spend time with your family now, you must not want it enough.'

"We are suggesting that coaches think differently: 'I need you to bring your whole person to the job. If you are out of balance, you are not going to be able to sustain your performance at the high level we need. Therefore, even if you have spurts of high achievement, you will be consistently underperforming.'

"This doesn't mean that you should never get in a player's face and tell him that his play or behavior is unacceptable. We're not saying that players should be undisciplined. We're saying that true discipline—real accountability, real responsibility—comes from

---

within. You, the coach, need to accept that, and so, in turn, do your players. If you've chosen right and if you've taught the right things, you can go to your kids and say, 'You know the program and you're not getting it done,' and they have to take responsibility for their own behavior. But if you have a system that depends on fear and intimidation, that doesn't teach accountability and responsibility, the players have a built-in excuse: 'I was only doing what you told me to do.' No accountability. No responsibility. No ownership.

"You've got to give the kids a chance to buy into the system. You teach, they learn. You teach, they learn. But at some point they have to account for their own actions. Not your demands—their own actions. If kids behave inappropriately, you have to confront them with the consequences, up to and including, if necessary, dismissal from the team. The choice then rests with the player, not the coach."

Self-definition, Professional Style

Kristina Koznick, by the age of twenty-two, had already been competing on the World Cup Circuit for seven years and won three U.S. slalom titles. Recurring injuries and the stress of world-class competition, however, were causing her to reevaluate her career in sports. In a story published in the Minneapolis *Star Tribune* on February 18, 1998, Koznick discussed with reporter Rachel Blount the process of self-examination that had led her to consider early retirement. (Italics have been added for emphasis.)

At the end of last season, Koznick realized that before she could give up skiing, she had to understand what it meant in her life. *She concluded that while it didn't define her as a person, it still made her happy.* She chose to ski for one more year and concentrate on all the things that made her love racing: the speed, the camaraderie, the thrill of challenging the mountain. Once she did that, the other side of the equation—the medals—fell in behind.

"Since I was 6 years old, I've been identified as the skier, as in, 'There's Kristina Koznick, the skier.' It got to the point where I was thinking I was a good person when I did well and a bad person when I didn't.

"I put so much pressure on myself to win that I wasn't having a good time. Now, I understand myself so much better. I love skiing; it's what I want to do. *This is my life, and I'm in control.*"

Some athletes—and coaches—are much older, or have sunk much lower, than Kristian Koznick before they realize they need to take control of their lives. Consider New Jersey Devils Defenseman Ken Daneyko, who had achieved about all hockey could offer, including a Stanley Cup, but nearly lost it all because of chronic alcoholism. Daneyko held a press conference after undergoing treatment for his disease. Some of his comments show just how much his life was defined by his sport:

"I felt empty, all gaps and voids. The only control in my life was hockey. I wasn't drinking to relieve the stress of hockey, it was hockey that took the pressure off the rest of my life. It was the reprieve, the three hours I didn't have to worry about responsibility, about being grown up.

"I loved everything about hockey; I thought it was the only reason I had to feel good about myself.

"You know, it's a cliché, one day at a time, but it's true and *I'm just at the beginning of a long process of finding out who I am.*"

For every Kristina Koznick and Ken Daneyko who are able to redefine themselves, there are thousands of athletes and coaches who continue to define themselves by what they do rather than who they are.

You're Not Crazy; It Really Is the System

Even if you have defined yourself by who you are and not what you do, you still must deal with "the system."

No, there isn't some gigantic conspiracy out there trying to drive you out of coaching, although that's not to say it doesn't seem that way at times. There is, however, a crazy world of changing rules, complicated institutional policies, and arbitrary administrative decisions that constitute the organized part of organized sports, and dealing with this world just might make you wish you had quit coaching. Even the best coaches are sometimes done in by the system, as *Collegiate Baseball* reported on June 5, 1998:

> Ken Schreiber was recently named high school "Co-Coach of the Century" by *Collegiate Baseball*. The LaPorte, Indiana, coach looked around at baseball's direction and decided, in the middle of the season, he wanted no more of it.
>
> "It was just a combination of 39 years in the profession. It's been a 365-day-a-year job. I will say it gets harder to coach because of outside distractions, such as Title IX, gender equity, AAU basketball, soccer, club sports, etc. If we could just coach the game 'between the lines,' it would be much simpler, and more pleasant. My health is fine, despite a flared-up ulcer. It's just the outside distractions."

RICK:

"Almost everyone in the coaching profession, at one time or another, feels some degree of frustration. Established coaches, young coaches, assistants—all tell me the same story: 'Rick, I just need some perspective. The administration is getting to me, the rules are getting to me, and the kids are getting to me. I need to know I'm not going nuts! Am I off base here?'"

Some coaches deal with their frustrations by moving around within the profession, often for legitimate reasons. While some coaches are happy to remain at an institution for most of their career—Joe Paterno has been at Penn State for forty-eight years—others move to enhance their careers. Coaches also move if the goals of the institution change in a direction they don't care to follow.

Other coaches seem more pointlessly nomadic, moving every couple of years in the futile hope of finding an answer to some of the distractions, disappointments, and problems of their current job.

We don't pretend to know, nor do we care to speculate, on the motives of basketball coach Pete Gillen for his career changes. He has had success and earned respect wherever he has been. His move from Providence College to the University of Virginia did generate some comments, which are illustrative of the frustrations of many in the profession. The following is excerpted from an article in the *Providence Journal-Bulletin*. Once again, we've added italics for emphasis.

> When Pete Gillen left the security of Xavier for Providence, he wanted the ultimate challenge.
>
> Gillen spoke of always wondering what it would be like "playing the best," something he couldn't do at Xavier.
>
> Once Gillen settled into the Providence job, *reality hit. Recruiting was difficult* and he quickly loaded up on junior-college players and high-school stars with baggage who struggled academically. *School administrators were often difficult to deal with. The academic tutoring department was in flux.*
>
> "At any school, no one knows completely what's going on until you get there," Gillen said. He tried to change many things at Providence *but felt his head hitting against the proverbial stone wall too often.* He had problems with academic tutoring, admissions, sometimes with his schedule.
>
> "There were wonderful people at Providence who treated me

great. *My point is, No coach is happy, because of the system.* You're fighting AAU people, parents, your players act up [and] you're on the hook."

The final blow in the Gillen-Providence relationship came over his contract, which had recently been substantially extended. After the run to the '97 Final Eight, Providence officials denied Gillen permission to speak to other schools. He publicly said he was "very happy at Providence," but privately seethed. Not letting him talk to a school [Virginia] that offered a more lucrative position is nearly unheard of in coaching circles, where nearly everyone is granted permission to explore jobs that offer more money and/or prestige.

JOHN:
"For me, this is the crux of what this book is all about. As a coach, you have to know when to stay and when to leave. Sometimes you have to be really blunt with yourself and say, 'You know what? It is the place. If I stay here, I'm dead. I have to leave.' Other times you will find coaches just running from one spot to another, trying to avoid the problems that exist everywhere.

"In my own career, I've been tempted several times to leave Minnesota because I thought another program might have more to offer. But when I investigated these opportunities, I always found that, while there may be advantages to another university's approach, there were always disadvantages, too. Sometimes you think if you can just go to another place, you won't have problems. Well, there are problems everywhere—not the same problems in every case, but real problems nonetheless.

"Remember the story of Angela, the softball catcher? Just as some players think a transfer will solve all their problems, some coaches think they can run away from trouble.

"It's just my opinion, but I really think Pete Gillen found out he was beating his head against a wall at Providence, and he needed to leave. In this type of situation, a coach needs to have the courage and the clarity of vision to see that it's a 'me or them' situation. When the 'them' is an institution, it is usually the coach who needs to protect his or her sanity by making a change.

"There are things about my institution that I don't like, but there are also a lot of things I do like. A few years ago, I spent too much of my time trying to change things I had no control over. It was driving me nuts and damn near drove me out of coaching. I've had to learn the limits of my influence—what I can change and what I can't change. The way things are now, I prefer to stay where I am. I'm enthusiastic about my job again. If my university were to change its policies radically, I might have to reevaluate my position. Even if that happened, though, the system isn't going to drive me crazy or out of coaching.

"The coaches who are staying in the game and thriving are the ones who have figured out how to take care of themselves. They know where they are in their professional development and what is appropriate for them to do. I got a note recently from my former assistant, who is now a Division I head coach. He said he felt more alive than he had in a long time. I'm sure the decision he made to move up in his career was appropriate. He made it because he wanted to, not because he needed to. His decision not only affected his career, but mine as well. His leaving has made my job fresh and different. I've had to take on new responsibilities.

"Sometimes a coach can't grow unless he or she leaves one job for another. Sometimes a coach can be reinvigorated in his or her current position. Either way, the survivors and thrivers call their own shots for their own reasons and interests."

Rick:

"What has happened since John's assistant left has indicated to me that there is now a healthy system in place here. It's adaptable, it's flexible, it's growing. It's not static and stale.

"John's former assistant coach is rising to the challenge of being a head coach. John is excited, his other long-time assistant is happy and productive, and the players have taken on more responsibility."

Some Final Thoughts

The Lonely Coach

One of the fallacies of leadership is the notion that a leader should be able to "do it all." In fact, the more leadership you take on, the more you need to realize that, while a leader can do a lot, no leader can do everything. Good leaders recognize their limitations; they empower others and delegate responsibility.

Some coaches have a tough time empowering others and delegating responsibility. They feel that, since they are the ones who will ultimately be held accountable for the success or failure of the program, they should personally do everything "important" and even micromanage the "unimportant" stuff they have delegated. This type of coach will sooner or later have to deal with feelings of isolation and loneliness."

RICK:

"As the head coach, whom do you have to turn to for advice about coaching? You have lots of people around you on the field, but they are your subordinates— assistants or players. They don't see things from your perspective. Your family doesn't understand your job well enough to offer specific, situational advice about coaching. All they can offer is general comfort and support. No wonder so many coaches feel isolated and lonely.

"One of the reasons for bringing a 'head–head coach' into a program is to deal with such feelings of isolation and loneliness. A trained psychologist who also is an integral part of an athletic program can offer informed, unbiased, straightforward, and non-judgmental advice to a head coach.

"If, as in most programs, you don't have access to this kind of professional resource, one of the best things you can do is to form an informal support group of fellow head coaches within your institution or organization.

"Or you might consider joining an association of peers: coaches in your sport at your level from other institutions and organizations. Such groups have regional and national meetings and con-ferences, and offer professional support to their members.

"Some coaches have trouble sharing problems with those they consider direct competitors. But when it comes to dealing with The Other Stuff, other coaches are not competitors. They are colleagues who share many of the same problems. Never underestimate the importance of networking with your peers."

LOOKING IN THE MIRROR CAN BE TERRIFYING

Yes, there is risk in self-examination and change. But there is substantial-ly more risk in doing the same destructive things over and over again.

JOHN:

"I was scared to death when I was forced to take a hard look at myself. It's not pleasant to have to examine yourself not only as a coach but as a husband, father, friend, and all the other components of your whole personality.

"For me, self-examination is working. If I hadn't started the process with myself, there is no way the program could have changed. If I hadn't changed myself, I don't believe my family situation would be as stable and happy as it is today.

"I have defined myself in a totally different way. This new definition has enabled me to have a better relationship with my staff and players. Now, instead of distrust and silence, there is mutual respect and communication. And because I'm spending much less time and energy dealing with The Other Stuff, I can focus more on the issues that will help us become a better team."

WE'RE STILL IN IT TO WIN

Our goal in writing this book has been to help you, the coach, perform at your highest level for the longest period of time. We believe that there is a direct correlation between your performance and the performance of your players: your players will perform optimally only when you are performing optimally. And when your players perform at their best, you win more games, which, really, is still the bottom line in competitive sports.

Reading one book isn't in itself going to turn you into a good coach or keep you in the game. But if you've seen something of yourself in these pages, and if, as a result, you've called a "time-out" to examine who you are and what you're doing as a coach, then our effort has been a success.